weights for women

MITCHELL BEAZLEY

weights for women

yolande green

Weights for Women
by Yolande Green

First published in Great Britain in 2004 by Mitchell Beazley,
an imprint of Octopus Publishing Group Limited,
2-4 Heron Quays, London E14 4JP.

ISBN 1 84000 859 8

A CIP catalogue record for this book is available from the British Library.

Publisher's note: Before following any advice or exercises contained in
this book, it is recommended that you consult your doctor if you suffer
from any health problems or special conditions. The publisher cannot
accept responsibility for any injuries or damage incurred as a result of
following the advice given in this book.

Commissioning Editor Vivien Antwi, Kate John
Executive Art Editor Christine Keilty
Project Editor Naomi Waters
Design Peter Gerrish
Photography Ruth Jenkinson
Production Gilbert Francourt
Editor Mary Lambert
Proofreader Siobhan O' Connor
Indexer Hilary Bird

Typset in Caslon, Universe and Vectora
Printed and bound in China

Contents

Introduction

Weight training has helped many people to increase muscle tone, lose weight and change their shape, along with developing better concentration and movement control, all of which have helped to improve performance in their daily tasks. Others report feeling greater self-awareness, a deeper sense of wellbeing, greater self-esteem and better health. After a few weeks of following an exercise programme, people often say that they've slept better, feel stronger and have more energy to cope with day-to-day life.

Whether you are a beginner to strength training (also referred to as weight training or weight lifting) or someone who is already advanced in the practice, needing alternative exercises to add variety, increase intensity or overcome a frustrating plateau, the *Weights for Women* exercises in this book will help you develop your own programme step-by-step. It will educate you in the safest and most effective ways to strength train.

Many people don't realize the numerous benefits of a sound strength-training programme. Weight training has been shown to: tone the muscles, increasing muscle size only if desired; build muscle, tendon, bone, and ligament strength; increase physical performance and improve appearance; increase metabolic efficiency and decrease the risk of injury.

The *Weights for Women* training programme provides clear exercise instructions and customized strength-training programmes that will allow you to achieve the results you desire. You can follow them either at home or in your gym.

Over the years it has been clearly established that people who engage in some form of physical activity, either by lifestyle or occupation, are likely to live longer and healthier lives. Research shows that burning even a modest amount of calories from increased physical activity has a significant impact on how long you live.

Regular exercise is also likely to help reduce a number of risk factors to your health. When it is combined with a weight plan, exercise is likely to help you stay on a diet and lose weight. Regular exercise is also associated with a reduction in blood pressure, improved glucose regulation, promotion of better lipid profiles (body fat) and stronger and denser bones.

Taking the first step

Before you begin this exercise programme, take a few minutes to read through the following questions. This physical activity readiness questionnaire (PAR-Q) taken from the American College of Sports Medicine (ACSM) guidelines will help determine your suitability for starting an exercise programme:

● Has your doctor ever said that you have a heart condition and that you should only participate in physical activity recommended by a doctor?

- Do you suffer from any pain in your chest during physical activity?
- In the past month, have you felt any chest pain when you were not doing physical activity?
- Do you lose your balance because of dizziness, or do you ever lose consciousness?
- Do you have a bone or joint problem that could be made worse by a change in your level of physical activity?
- Is your doctor currently prescribing drugs for your blood pressure or a heart condition?
- Do you know of any other reason why you should not participate in regular physical activity?

If you answered 'yes' to one or more of these questions, if you are over 40 years of age and have been inactive in recent months, or if you are at all concerned about your general state of health, do consult a doctor before continuing with the exercise programme detailed in this book.

If you answered 'no' to each of the above questions, it should be safe for you to go ahead with the book's exercise programme.

A complete physical exercise programme

There are three principal components to a rounded programme of physical exercise – these are aerobic exercise, strength exercise, and flexibility training. It is not essential that all three components be performed during the same workout session; however, it is important to include all three in your normal weekly exercise programme.

Weights for Women covers two of these main areas: strength exercise and flexibility training. To achieve all-round fitness, it is also essential to include some form of aerobic exercise. This doesn't mean you have to attend an aerobics class. You could try walking briskly for 20 minutes, going up and down the stairs for 20 minutes, or doing a sport you enjoy such as swimming, cycling, or tennis. The key to aerobic exercise is to get slightly out of breath, but still be able to hold a conversation.

Making a commitment to a regular physical exercise programme is more important than the intensity of the workouts, so choose the exercises you believe you are likely to perform and enjoy. Exercise should become part of your lifestyle.

Why weights?

During the past few years, more and more studies have shown that sensible strength training produces many health and fitness benefits. Key research has shown the positive physiological responses to basic programmes of strength exercise. Below are 12 examples of the benefits that strength training provides for women.

1 Reduces muscles loss

Women who do not do strength training lose between 2.25 and 3kg (5 and 7lb) of muscle every decade. Although aerobic forms of exercise improve cardiovascular fitness, they do not prevent the loss of muscle tissue. Only doing strength exercise maintains our muscle mass and strength throughout our lives.

2 Prevents metabolic rate reduction

Muscles are very active tissue, so any muscle loss is accompanied by a reduction in our resting metabolism. Research has shown that the average adult experiences a 2 to 5 per cent reduction in metabolic rate every decade of their lives. Because regular strength exercise prevents muscle loss, it also prevents the accompanying decrease in resting metabolic rate. Metabolic rate is the rate at which your body is able to turn your food into energy, rather than depositing it as body fat.

3 Increases muscle mass

As most women do not perform strength exercise, they first need to replace the muscle tissue that has been lost through inactivity. Fortunately, research shows that a standard strength-training programme can increase muscle mass by about 1.4kg (3lb) over an eight-week training period. This is a typical training response for those women who do a 25-minute weights programme, three days a week.

4 Increases metabolic rate

Research shows that adding 1.4kg (3lb) of muscle increases a woman's metabolic rate by 7 per cent, and our daily calorie requirement by 15 per cent. When we are at rest, 0.45kg (1lb) of muscle requires about 35 calories per day for tissue maintenance, and during exercise muscle energy utilization increases dramatically. Women who replace muscle through sensible strength exercise use more calories all day long, even at rest, so they reduce the likelihood of putting on weight.

5 Reduces body fat

Research has proven that strength exercise can produce 1.8kg (4lb) of fat loss after three months of training, even though the subjects in question were eating 15 per cent more calories per day. That is, a basic strength-training programme resulted in 1.4kg (3lb) more lean weight, 1.8kg (4lb) less fat weight, and 370 more calories per day food intake.

6 Increases bone mineral density

The effects of progressive resistance exercise have similar effects on both muscle and bone tissue. The same training stimulates increased muscle myoproteins and mineral content. It has been demonstrated that significant increases in the bone mineral density of the upper femur (the top thigh bone) can occur after four months of strength exercise.

7 Improves glucose metabolism

A 23 per cent increase in glucose uptake after four months of strength training has also been reported. Poor glucose metabolism is associated with adult late-onset diabetes, so improved glucose metabolism is an important benefit of regular strength exercise.

8 Increases gastrointestinal transit time

One study showed a 56 per cent increase in gastrointestinal transit time (how fast food passes through the intestines) after three months of strength training. This is a significant finding because delayed gastrointestinal transit has been related to higher risks of colon cancer.

9 Reduces blood pressure

Strength training alone has been shown to significantly reduce resting blood pressure. A study revealed that strength training plus aerobic exercise is also effective for improving blood pressure. After two months of combined exercise, the participants saw a significant drop in their blood pressure.

10 Improves blood lipid levels

Research has shown that an improved blood lipid profile can be achieved after several weeks of doing strength exercise. This has been shown to help reduce high levels of cholesterol, which has been linked to the risk of heart attack.

11 Reduces lower back pain

Several years of research on strength training and back pain has shown that strong lower back muscles are less likely to be injured. One study found that patients with lower back problems had significantly less back pain after doing 10 weeks of specific (full-range) strength exercise.

12 Reduces arthritic pain

Sensible strength training has been found to ease the pain of osteoarthritis and rheumatoid arthritis in many sufferers. This is good news because most women who suffer from arthritis pain need strengthening exercise to develop stronger muscles, bones, and connective tissue.

Know your muscles

The best way to train your muscles is to overload them with resistance. Pushing a muscle just beyond its limits makes it work hard, with the fibres tearing slightly. In 48 hours, however it is healed and stronger.

Your muscles will quite quickly adapt to the extra challenge by developing more strength (the amount of force a muscle can produce) and more endurance (the ability to contract repeatedly over a period of time). The appearance of your muscles changes, too, as you start to develop muscle tone (how firm your muscles are) and definition (how sculpted they look).

Toning and defining muscles

You can develop muscle tone with any exercise. The firmer you want to be, however, the more you need to use greater resistance, using specific exercises to target key muscles.

Muscle definition can be harder to achieve for some people, as it depends on body fat levels. The leaner you are, the more sculptured your muscles will appear because less fat is filling out your curves.

Combining some calorie-burning exercise, such as walking, aerobics, or cycling, with your weight-training programme will make your body look more defined.

Long, slim muscles are considered to be the ideal shape, but unfortunately muscle shape is largely genetic. Also your skeletal structure (bones) plays a major role in determining how muscular you look. The weights you lift and the number of repetitions (reps) you do (see Planning your workouts, page 18) will determine whether you develop greater strength or greater endurance.

If you lift weights and then stop, any gains in performance will be noticeably lost after three to four weeks. So once you have reached your desired level, simply maintain it by following a regular programme for a minimum of three times a week.

The scientific view

Your muscular strength reflects the prime function of muscle – changing chemical energy into mechanical energy to generate force, perform work, and produce movement. In addition, muscle tissue stabilizes the body's position, regulates organ volume, generates heat, and propels fluids and food matter through the various body systems.

A muscle consists of individual muscle fibres bundled together and surrounded by three connective tissue layers. Muscles are connected to the bone by tendons, and bones are connected together by ligaments. Both are found at joints in the bone and are strengthened by weight training.

Oxygen consumption

During muscle contraction, there are increases in breathing effort and blood flow that enhance oxygen delivery to muscle tissue. After muscle contraction has stopped, deep breathing may continue until oxygen supplies are renewed. This is why it is important to breath continuously, rather than holding your breath, during exercise to enable the muscles to get enough oxygen to perform effective exercise.

Muscle fatigue

The inability of a muscle to contract forcefully after prolonged exercise is called 'muscle fatigue'. Fatigue results mainly from changes within the muscle fibres. Even before actual muscle fatigue occurs, a person may feel tired and want to stop. Training through muscle fatigue can lead to injury and potential long-term body damage, and should be avoided at all costs.

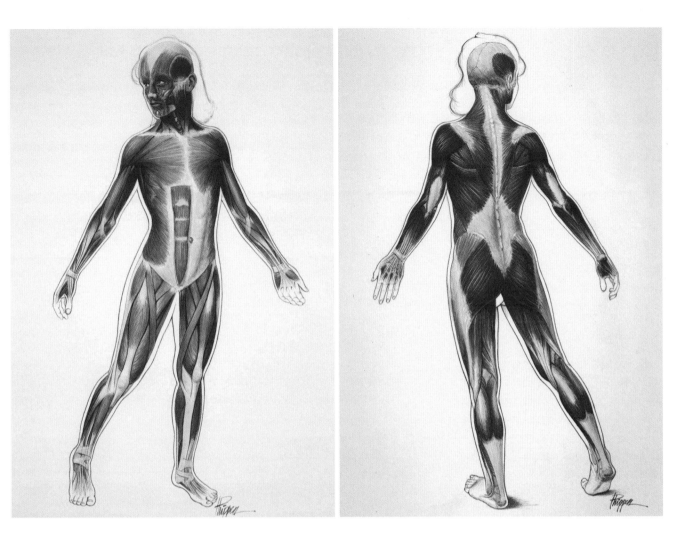

Ageing and muscle tissue

Ageing begins at about 30 years of age (a depressing thought). From this age onwards, people undergo a slow, progressive loss of skeletal muscle mass that is replaced largely by fibrous connective tissue and adipose tissue (fat). In part this decline is often due to increasing inactivity. Accompanying the loss of muscle mass is a decrease in the maximum strength achieved, a slowing of muscle reflexes, and a loss of flexibility. However, all these processes can generally be slowed by starting a regular exercise programme.

The stretch reflex

Muscle fibres contain sensory nerve endings called muscles spindles the main function of which is to send messages back from the muscle to inform the brain about its state of stretch.

If the muscle is over-stretched, distortion of the central part of the muscle spindle causes the stretch reflex automatically to come into play to contract the muscle and avoid any damage through tearing – this is that feeling of tightness when performing a stretch.

The amount and rate of contraction which come from the stretch reflex are proportional to the amount and rate of stretch, hence the faster and more forceful the stretch, the faster and more forceful the reflex contraction of the stretched muscle and a higher likelihood of the muscle tearing.

When you stretch, work to the level of the stretch reflex. Hold it until you feel the muscle slightly tighten, then maintain it a bit longer and slowly the stretch reflex will switch off, allowing you to take the stretch a little further until the stretch reflex switches on again (see Warming up, pages 20–21).

The muscles of the body

The exercises in this book are designed to train specific muscle groups. At the beginning of each section on a particular muscle group you will find a segment of the above drawings enlarged to show the muscles you will be working with.

Posture and alignment

Maintaining a good posture during exercise is the most important factor when training. In fact, it is more important than how much weight you are lifting or how many repetitions or sets you are doing.

Good posture, also known as neutral alignment, is a way of describing a position where your body can function most effectively. It is a position that allows the body to have its most natural length and for all muscles, joints, and bones to sit in their natural position, not rotated, twisted, or compressed.

If you train a muscle or several muscles groups when your body is not in neutral alignment, or a good posture, you are risking injury to your joints and muscles. This is because if the joint, muscle, or ligament is not sitting or lying in its neutral alignment (or most desired position) you could put extensive pressure on it which causes either short-term or long-term damage.

Posture and the internal organs

Another reason why good posture is so important is that it allows our internal organs to function efficiently. For example, when we sit in a slumped position, our digestive system cannot work efficiently. Try this: sit in a slumped position and breathe in through your nose and out through your mouth, making the breath last as long as you can and count how many breaths you can do this for. Now stand up tall, chest proud, head slightly lifted, shoulders back and down, and repeat the breathing sequence again. You should find that in an elongated position you are able to breathe more deeply and for longer – this is because your lungs and rib cage are more open and have a fuller capacity to work.

So what is good posture?

If you looked at yourself in a mirror side on, with your left shoulder facing the mirror, the following alignment is ideal. You can also get someone to take a photo of you standing side on:

Head: Keep it in a neutral position, not tilted forward or back, with your ears in line with shoulders, chin not jutting out and your eyes looking slightly up as if looking over the horizon.

Shoulders: Draw back and down away from your ears, allowing your chest to be lifted and proud.

Upper spine: Maintain a normal curve and be slightly rounded and forward.

Scapulae (shoulder blades) : Keep flat against upper back – check they aren't pushing out.

Middle of spine: Maintain a normal curve, ie almost flat.

Lumbar spine: Maintain a normal curve that is slightly curved in.

Pelvis: Keep in a neutral position with your bottom not sticking out or tucked under. Feel your pelvic bones at the top of your hips and make sure they don't feel tilted forward or back.

Knee joints: Keep in a neutral position, so that they are neither flexed nor hyperextended, which means not bent forward or locked back.

Ankle joints: Keep in a neutral position, with your leg vertical and at a right angle to the sole of your foot.

Looking at your posture takes practice, and finding your neutral position should be done in every position you adopt. Follow these exercises to help you find your neutral position; practise them in front of a mirror to guide you.

Finding neutral when standing

Stand with your feet hip-width apart – your toes will want to turn out very slightly. Roll your pelvis forward and back – do this by tucking your bottom under, then sticking it out. Now try to find a point in between where your bottom isn't tucked under or sticking out. Draw in your lower abdominal muscles, and lengthen up as if you were trying to stretch out the creases in your T-shirt. Lift your chest, slide your shoulders back and down. Balance your head so that it is central over your neck and ears, and in line with your shoulders. Look ahead to just over the horizon.

Finding neutral when sitting

Sit on a chair or stool, first making sure it is not too high or too low. To find the correct height, have both feet firmly on the floor, hip-width apart, with your knees only a few inches lower than your hips. Imagine balancing a tray on your lap: if you are too low it would slide off your knees; if the tray would tip into your stomach, your knees are too high. Sit tall in the chair, don't lean against the back, just sit slightly forward. Now roll your pelvis forward and back as in the above exercise, and feel the way this changes your posture, especially your spinal position. Then find a position where you have a small curve in your lower back and your hip bones feel level. Draw in your lower abdominals and lengthen the area. Lift your chest and draw your shoulders down as above, position your head centrally over your neck, and raise your eyes.

Finding neutral on all fours

Kneel on a mat, with your knees hip-width apart, placing your hands at shoulder-width in front of you. Keep your hands directly under your shoulders not too far forward – the distance between your shoulders and hips should be the same as the distance between your hands and knees. Roll your pelvis forward and back, a bit like a cat stretching, drawing out through the lower curve in your spine, then gently increase the size of the curve almost making a dip in your lower back. Stop in the middle where you feel it is almost flat, with a small dip in your lower back, where your bottom is not sticking up or tucked under. Draw your shoulders back and down, keep your neck long and your eyes looking down. Draw your chin to your chest, but without giving yourself a double chin.

How posture can improve the way you look

Just working on your posture can improve the way you look. Think of an outfit you used to wear that made you feel really good and flattered your shape. Imagine holding yourself in this outfit, and practice this exercise in a mirror and watch your changing shape.

Let your shoulders drop forward, your chest collapse, and your body sink into itself. Do your breasts look toned and perky? Now try standing tall as in the exercises above, and see the difference to your breasts. It is very common for women who are conscious of their breasts to adopt a poor posture, but this just makes the breasts sag more, making them look bigger than they actually are.

Try this second exercise. Increase the curve in your lower back by sticking your bottom out, although this makes your bottom look very firm it looks bigger because of the curve in your lower back, which can cause lower back pain. Now tuck your bottom under – imagine that you have a long swishing tail and you are tucking it between your legs. Look at the shape and tone of your bottom, does it look soft and flat? Find a point in between for a perfect look.

Posture and weight training

Before you do any of the exercises in the book, for example, if you are on all fours performing push-ups or standing to perform bicep curls, always do a quick posture check, from your feet upwards or head down, to make sure that your:

● feet are a hip-width apart
● knees aren't locked
● pelvis is in a neutral position
● abdominals are drawn in
● lower back has a small curve
● chest is open
● shoulders are down
● ears are in line with your shoulders
● eyes are looking up

Weight training

Many women insist that they don't want to have prominent muscles, but, if you want curves, you also need toned muscles. Muscles don't have to mean you have the bulk or bulges of a body builder, but they are the key to sculpting shape, definition, and body tone.

Selecting free weights

Using free weights in your exercise programme can be a safe and effective means of improving your strength and fitness. They provide a stimulus for muscle fitness development, which can increase the amount of calories you burn (body fat reduction), improve muscle size, and enhance muscle strength, power, and endurance.

Before beginning your exercise programme, think about the equipment you will need:

Free weights come in two basic types:
Barbells are long bars 1.2–1.8m (4–6ft) wide (average weight about 4kg (9lb)) with weights attached or slots to add weight plates of your choice. Always secure with collars to stop the weights slipping off.
Dumbbells are smaller, single, hand-held weights which come in different sizes from 1kg–80kg (2¼lb–176lb). Start off with the smaller weights and increase them as you get stronger.

In this book we have used a variety of the above, but there are alternatives. Instead of a barbell, for example, we have used a **body bar**. This is a set weight bar, available from most fitness equipment stockists. You can also use a weighted bar or pole that you may have at home.

Instead of using dumbbells you can fill old water bottles with sand, water, or lentils, or use tins or bags of sugar to the weights given above.

The handles of the free weights need to be comfortable to enable a good grip, and they should not cause undue muscle fatigue when you are lifting them. Practise some exercises with the weights before beginning your full programme.

Different grips

The two main grips used in this book are the under-grip (see Concentrate curls, page 67), where the hand grasps the bar from underneath with your palms facing upward. The other grip is the over-grasp (see Military press, page 57), where you pick up the bar, placing your hands over the bar with your palms facing down. You could also try a combination grip, which is one hand over and one hand under.

Other equipment

Dynabands are rubber bands that come in different resistances, so try them out before you buy to see what types you want. A towel can sometimes be substituted – although it doesn't have the same resistance qualities of a band – but make sure that it is long enough to grip well.
Fitness steps come in different shapes and sizes, generally with detachable blocks to alter the height and incline. The bottom step of a staircase (make sure it is wide enough) can be used if you do not want to buy a fitness step.
Benches if you have the opportunity to use a bench, try to use one that adjusts in height and back rest.
Stability ball great for any exercise programme, make sure that it is anti burst and ask for the maximum load if you wish to lie on it and use weights.

Injuries

Before starting your programme, it is important to read through the checklist (PAR-Q) in the introduction (see pages 6–7). If you have any recent injuries, do consult a doctor before attempting to perform any of the exercises.

If you have had an injury in the past and have now recovered, you may still need to make slight adjustments to the exercises you do to prevent over-stress on that area of your body, otherwise this could lead to that injury flaring up again.

Below some common injury problems are covered, but remember, if you already have an injury, exercise can be an excellent way to help improve the condition and regain movement, balance, and control. However, if you over-exercise, or put too much strain on the weak joint or muscle, you could cause further problems, so always speak to your doctor first and find out how much you can do.

Lower back pain

Many orthopaedic specialists consider muscular weakness, particularly in the abdominal region, and poor joint flexibility in the back and legs as primary factors that lead to lower back pain. Both muscle strengthening and joint flexibility exercises are commonly prescribed for prevention of and rehabilitation from chronic lower back strain. Even continuing normal daily activities, within the limits dictated by the pain suffered, leads to a more rapid recovery from an episode of acute back pain than bed rest. Following a resistance-training programme provides an excellent means for strengthening the abdomen and lumbar extensor muscles of the lower back through their full range of motion. These muscles provide the support and protection necessary for the spine. However, a considerable strain can be put on the lower spine if exercises are not performed properly, so follow the guidelines for each exercise, maintain a good posture, and let your legs take the strain, not your back, when picking up weights.

Calf injuries

The main causes of injuries to these muscles are when they become weak, inflexible, and short from aerobics, running, lack of stretching, or wearing high heels.

If you have suffered an injury, try to decrease your level of aerobic training, and make sure your footwear is correct and supportive, both in your sports and everyday shoes. Always include plenty of calf stretches in your exercise routine (see page 24).

Knee problems

These type of injuries are normally caused by trauma, such as a motor accident, over-use from running, high-impact exercise, or moving and twisting exercises with one foot fixed on the ground. Try to reduce your exercise programme, avoid high-impact movements, and build up the thigh muscles through weight training as shown in this book. Focus on your posture when exercising as this may be increasing your knee problems. Make sure you're not knock-kneed, as this throws 80 per cent of stress on to your inner knee. Work on flexibility and strength exercises in your hamstrings and quadriceps (see pages 30–37).

Remember, if you feel a sudden pain mid-workout, stop at once; if you carry on you could increase any damage that has occurred.

The essential step-by-step training guide

This step-by-step guide will help you to learn different weight-training exercises and to achieve a full, all-round workout. It is planned for three training days a week, all of which can be done within your home environment or the gym. Start off as a beginner. If, after the first week, you find you have completed these exercises with ease, move on to the intermediate level and then, when you have more confidence, progress to the advanced level.

You can mix and match the different exercises, and the idea of working through the workout from beginner to advanced will enable you to learn the moves in progressive stages.

Try to keep the exercises grouped as I have put them, but feel free to mix them up. For example, you can use a beginner level for quads and hamstrings, and advanced level for glutes.

'Rep' is short for repetition. This means how many times you lift the weights. 'Set' means a group of repetitions – for example, 15 reps x 3 sets means lifting the weight 15 times in three groups. Always rest approximately one to two minutes between sets of each exercise, or long enough to catch your breath. The reps and sets given are only a guideline. Think to yourself: 'is my body being challenged without me losing control of my posture and technique' and decide accordingly.

Choosing the right weight

The easiest guide is to do 15 repetitions with your chosen weight (see page 14). If you find 15 easy and feel you could do another five or more, your weight is too light. Ideally, you should start to feel the weight challenging you from around 12–15 repetitions. However, if you get to 10 and you are really struggling, you are using too much weight. Once you have worked out the correct weight to start with, try to keep that weight for the rest of your sets. Over a period of time, ie a few weeks, you will feel your muscles becoming stronger and fitter, and you will be able to increase the weights slightly.

Safety guidelines

Free weights such as barbells and dumbbells require far more muscular coordination than resistance machines. Because the movement is not restricted, the risk of injury is higher, so maintain a good grip, a stable position either standing or sitting, use good technique and form, and follow the exercise instructions.

When lifting weights off the floor, and down again, always lift using your legs and not your back. Most accidents occur when an insecure weight falls on a body part or when a dumbbell is dropped.

Do not lift too much weight on your own; with heavy weights, ask a partner to help you.

Planning your workouts

The American College of Sports Medicine (ACSM) suggests that people exercise for 3–5 days weekly, with a 5–10-minute warm-up before the main workout of 30–45 minutes. A further 5–10 minutes stretching to cool down is suggested, so follow all these guidelines when doing your workout programme.

Using free weights as in the exercises in this book can develop muscle fitness in different ways – strength, endurance, or power – depending on the number of repetitions and sets you do.

For muscle power – do 3–5 reps and 1–3 sets
For muscle strength – do 5–8 reps and 1–3 sets
For muscle endurance – do 15–20 reps and 1–3 sets

Muscle groups to train
Always include exercises that work the following body areas in your workout to develop overall fitness:

Upper body: biceps, triceps, shoulder muscles, chest and upper back muscles
Torso: abdominal, oblique and lower back muscles
Legs: quadriceps, hamstrings, calf and buttock muscles

Day one – legs

LEVEL	MAJOR MUSCLE	EXERCISE	PAGE NO	REPS	SETS	COMMENTS
Beg	Quads	Squat with body bar	36	8–10	1	Perform with bar to begin with
Beg	Hamstrings	Hamstring curl on all fours	32	10 each leg	1	Vary arm position if necessary
Beg	Glutes	Gluteus lift	39	8 each side	1–2	Vary arm position if necessary
Beg	Calves	Single leg calf raise	44	10	1	Do both together if necessary
Beg	Adductor	Single leg lift	47	10	1	Vary arm position if necessary
Beg	Abductor	Single leg lift	51	10	1	Vary arm position if necessary
Int	Quads	Leg extension with dynaband	37	10–12	2	
Int	Hamstrings	Single leg stretch with ball	33	12 each leg	2	
Int	Glutes	Step and extend	41	12 each leg	2	
Int	Calves	Calf raise on step	43	12	2	Single or double legs
Int	Adductor	Squat and cross	49	12	2	
Int	Abductor	Narrow squat and lift	53	12	2	
Adv	Quads	Single leg bench squat	35	15 each leg	2–3	
Adv	Hamstrings	Lunge with body bar	31	15 each leg	2–3	
Adv	Glutes	X-tuck	40	15 each leg	2–3	Vary arm position if necessary
Adv	Calves	Down dog	45	12	2	
Adv	Adductor	Drop and catch	48	15	3	
Adv	Abductor	Side leg with band	52	15	3	

Starting your programme

Warm-up

Begin with 10-15 minutes of moderate cardiovascular activity, such as a brisk walk or jog (see page 21), before doing the warm-up stretches (see pages 21–27).

Cool-down

Stretch all the muscles you have worked. Hold each stretch for 30 seconds (see pages 22–27).

The main workout programme

I have devised beginner, intermediate, and advanced programmes for 30 minutes, three times a week. There is also an express 40-minute workout (see pages 82–85) for people who can only train once a week.

Beg = **beginner** – someone who hasn't exercised before or in the past two years

Int = **Intermediate** – someone who has exercised in the past two years at least once a week

Adv = **advanced** – someone who is already following a regular exercise programme more than once a week

These programmes are just basic plans. Once you have begun to work through the moves, mix and match, and add a few more exercises for each muscle group, if you have the time and to give you variety.

Day two – arms and torso

LEVEL	MAJOR MUSCLE	EXERCISE	PAGE NO	REPS	SETS	COMMENTS
Beg	Bicep	Standing curl	68	8–10	1	
Beg	Tricep	Push-up	63	10	1	Vary levels accordingly
Beg	Abs	Basic crunch	75	10	1	Vary arms
Beg	Obliques	Crunch twist	79	10	1	Vary arms
Int	Bicep	Hammer curl	69	12	2	
Int	Tricep	Triceps dip	65	12	2	Vary positions accordingly
Int	Abs	Reverse curl	76	12	2	Vary levels
Int	Obliques	Hip stacked lift	80	12	2	
Adv	Bicep	Concentrate curl	67	15	3	
Adv	Tricep	Triceps extension	64	15	3	Use either dumbells or bar
Adv	Abs	Plank	77	10	2	Vary levels
Adv	Obliques	Cycle	81	15	3	

Day three – back and chest

LEVEL	MAJOR MUSCLE	EXERCISE	PAGE NO	REPS	SETS	COMMENTS
Beg	Back	One-arm row	56	10	1	
Beg	Shoulders	Frontal raise	60	10	1	
Beg	Chest	Body-bar press	72	10	1	
Int	Back	Military press	57	12	2	
Int	Shoulders	Lateral raise	61	12	2	
Int	Chest	Fly	71	12	2	Flat or incline
Adv	Back	Seated row with dynaband	55	15	3	
Adv	Shoulders	Reverse fly	59	15	3	
Adv	Chest	Pec deck	73	15	3	

Warming up

The warm-up is one of the most important parts of your exercise programme. If you fail to warm up properly, you can increase the risk of injury and also reduce the results gained from the main workout.

The purpose of a warm-up

It is important to stretch before you begin your programme and to do cool-down stretches at the end. Start with some exercises that will make you warm, and try to do these for 10–15 minutes.

Stretch well, doing holding stretches of all the muscle groups that you are going to be using for about 10 seconds (see pages 22–27).

Also remember that stretching at the end of the workout is essential to avoid muscle damage. This time hold the stretches for all the muscle groups used for a bit longer – ideally up to 30 seconds (see pages 22–27).

As this is the start of your programme, make sure that you are wearing comfy, stretch clothing, such as T-shirt and shorts or leggings, and supportive trainers during your workout. You may find you need a sweatshirt or cover-up when you are warming up or cooling down.

Ideally, always do your exercises on a fitness mat, the thicker the better – yoga mats are very good because they do not slip.

The aim of the warm-up is to prepare your body for the stress of muscle overload that occurs during a weights programme. The emphasis is placed on warming up the muscles and raising the deep muscle temperature, so that the blood supply is increased to the working muscles. Joint mobility and lubrication are also aided by the extra flow of synovial fluid, which is produced in a healthy joint to help the joint function and to prevent infection or damage. It is also important in the warm-up to establish the right posture and to increase gradually the range of motion, ie how big the movement is around a joint. Examples of general warm-up exercises include riding a bike, a

brisk walk or a light jog, or possible low-impact exercises (see page 21).

The other part of the warm-up is the flexibility exercises. The muscles that are going to be worked during the session should function at an optimal level.

As muscles can be damaged if they are stretched when cold, always do a general warm-up first (see above). Always perform warm-up stretches before exercising any of the major muscle groups, and do them all if you do a full programme (see pages 18–19).

The benefits of stretching

There are many benefits that can be gained from stretching your muscles before a workout:

Increases the length of muscle – allows greater movement at the joint.

Injury prevention – a greater range of movement around a joint decreases the chances of injury in situations where joints may be forced.

Decreases muscle tightening – exercises can cause muscle tightness. This tightness can be reduced by stretching at the end of the workout.

Reduces muscle soreness – muscle soreness is often felt after a workout, though not always immediately; it sometimes appears after two or three days. Stretches can help to reduce any soreness in muscles.

Counteracts the shortening effect of weight training – the constant contracting of muscles during a heavy weight-training session can cause them to shorten in length. Stretching them lets them lengthen again.

Increases coordination between muscle groups – neuromuscular function improves with flexibility.

Improves muscular imbalances and postural alignment – stretching exercises can help to rectify some muscular imbalances and poor posture.

Increases speed and power of movement – the improved neuromuscular function achieved by stretching improves muscle function.

Helps muscle and general relaxation – in general stretching promotes muscle relaxation.

Improves body awareness – stretching specific muscles helps you to focus on them.

Static stretching

This is the gradual stretching of a muscle to a point where it is held, without bouncing, for 10 seconds. The muscle should be taken to a point where there is a feeling that it is being stretched or slightly tightened, but the position is comfortable – this is known as the 'stretch reflex' (see pages 10–11). If it is taken to a point of discomfort, ease off the stretch.

Static stretching, used in this book, is a safe way of stretching muscles and connective tissue because it involves no sudden movements. Always do these stretches after your cardiovascular warm-up (see below).

Static stretching is best suited for:
- general stretching of all muscles
- the early stages of recovery from injury
- the cool-down phase following a vigorous programme.

Indoor warm-up

These are two great ways to warm up indoors before starting your weights programme.

Running on the spot: March on the spot, using your arms in a power-walking action. Slowly take this to a brisker walk and, if you feel able, a slight jog. Try to maintain a good posture while jogging on the spot, and use a variety of techniques, such as bringing your knees up as high as you can, keeping your knees low but running fast on the spot, or kicking your heels to your buttocks.

Jumping jacks: These warm up the whole body and can be combined with jogging on the spot or done separately. Jump your legs apart, then bring your feet back together in the centre. Keep going with this move, jumping out and in, then try to add in your arms. As your feet go out, open your arms out to the side; as they come back in, bring your arms back in to your side.

Try to do this for about three minutes, if possible, or combine it with jogging on the spot. Avoid jumping on a concrete floor as it is too hard. A wooden floor is best as it has some give in it.

Outdoor warm-up

If you have the opportunity to warm up outside, take advantage of it. Here are some great exercises that can be done either in a local park or in the garden if you have room.

Walking: Go for a brisk walk. If you want to train a little harder, carry some hand weights with you (see page 14). As you walk, try to take long strides, and power with your arms. Think about your posture: stand tall and proud as you walk. Try to keep your pace consistent throughout your walk. To be a bit more competitive, try overtaking everyone in the park, or keep up with someone else who is walking a little faster than you. Try to make sure that you walk for at least five minutes.

Lunging: This is not only a great way to warm up the whole body, but it also works the thighs and buttocks. Start with both feet together, take a large step forward, and as you step forward allow your back knee to drop towards the floor. Step together again, then step forward with the other leg etc. Imagine you are trying to walk in the footprints of a giant or a dinosaur. Remember posture is important, so stand tall and maintain neutral alignment. To make the exercise a bit harder, try doing this with some hand weights (see page 14). Try to lunge for about five minutes – if you have a long hallway or garden you may be able to do this at home.

Using the stairs: One of the simplest warm-up exercises that can make a difference to your fitness, is always to use the stairs when you are out. Yes, an escalator looks easier, but really the stairs will make you feel better.

Use stairs as a simple warm-up exercise. Find some stairs local to you, perhaps in a nearby park, or simply use the stairs at home, as long as they are hazard-free, and include them in your inside warm-up. Walk briskly up and down the stairs, being as light on your feet as possible. If you want to work a little harder, try doing this with some hand weights (see page 14). Walk up and down the stairs continuously for about five minutes, if you can.

Hamstring stretch

This exercise stretches your hamstrings – the muscles at the back of your thighs. They often get quite tight just through daily use, so it is very important to stretch these muscles regularly.

1 Lie on your mat or on your step, if you have one (see page 14). Place your hands behind the back of your left knee and gently hug your knee towards your chest. Keep your right leg bent with the foot on the floor, keeping this foot close to your buttocks to support your lower back.

2 Lift up and lengthen your left leg towards the ceiling. Keep your leg as straight as possible – do not bend your knee too much, unless it feels uncomfortable. Hold your leg either above or below the knee, but not on the knee joint itself. Your hips and buttocks should stay on the mat/step, and avoid rotating your hips. Breathe steadily, and, as you start to feel the stretch reflex (see page 11), try to bring your leg closer towards your chest without bending your knee, then release back to the start position.

HOLD FOR 10 SECONDS ON BOTH SIDES

KEY POINTS

The further you take your hands towards your foot, the greater the stretch. Initially place your hands where you can maintain the stretch well, ideally with your hands behind the top of your thigh, closer to your buttocks.

1

2

Quadricep stretch

This exercise stretches the quadriceps – the muscles at the front of your thighs.

1 Stand upright and take your right foot in your right hand and stretch your leg back towards your buttocks. Keep your left knee slightly bent so you don't put too much pressure on your knee; your chest should be open and your shoulders relaxed, then release back to the start position.

2 If you find it difficult to balance during the exercise, stand next to a wall and rest your left hand on it to keep your balance. Try not to lean into the wall – just use it as support as you stretch the leg.

3 If you cannot reach your foot because of an injury or tight muscles, place a small towel or T-shirt across the front of your shin near the ankle. Holding both ends of the towel firmly, lift up your right foot.

HOLD FOR 10 SECONDS ON BOTH SIDES

KEY POINTS

Imagine your knees are stuck together or that you are holding a piece of paper between them. If you want to increase the stretch further, push your foot into your hand without moving your knee position. Be careful not to overstrain the muscle.

Gluteus stretch

This exercise stretches the gluteal muscles – the muscles in your buttocks.

1 This exercise does need some flexibility. If you find it difficult to perform, start with Step 1 of the hamstring stretch (see page 22), as this also stretches the gluteus muscles. Lie on your mat or your step with both feet on the floor. Place your left foot over your right knee, and your hands round the back of your right thigh. Take your left hand through the middle of your legs to clasp your right thigh. Ease your crossed legs up and towards your chest – the closer the legs come to the chest, the greater the stretch, but do not overdo it. Keep your shoulders relaxed and pressed into the step, with your elbows slightly bent. Release back to the start position.

HOLD FOR 10 SECONDS ON BOTH SIDES

KEY POINTS

If you find this exercise difficult, instead of clasping your thigh with your hands, use a towel or T-shirt. Place the towel behind the back of your right thigh, then hold on to both ends and lever your legs up towards your chest.

Calf stretch

This exercise stretches the calf muscles – the muscles in the lower part of your legs.

1 Stand with your feet together. Step forward into a straddle position. Lean forward, pushing your back heel into the floor until you feel the stretch. Release back to the start position.

2 Use a wall for support. Follow Step 1, but lean into the wall while pushing your back heel down.

3 To stretch further, use a step. Place your left foot on the step, put your right toe on the edge, then lengthen your right heel towards the floor until you feel the stretch in your calf muscle.

1

2

3

KEY POINTS

Keep your feet well apart and try not to lean too far forward over your knee joint. Step 3 is a deep stretch, and it takes balance to perform, so do only Steps 1 or 2 if you are just starting out.

HOLD FOR 10 SECONDS ON BOTH SIDES

Soleus stretch

As you sit down on your imaginary stool, imagine that the stool is slightly behind you and that you are perching on the edge of the stool. Keep a tall, upright posture as you do the stretch with your chest open.

HOLD FOR 10 SECONDS ON BOTH SIDES

This exercise stretches the soleus muscles – the muscles in your lower ankle.

1 Stand upright with both feet together, and place your right foot directly behind your left, so that your toe and heel are touching. Bend your knees, as if to sit on a stool, until you feel the stretch. If you don't, bend your knees a little more. Put your weight on your back right foot and not the front, so you can almost lift your front foot off the floor. Start by just lifting your toes to confirm that the weight is on the back foot and not the front. Release back to the start position.

2 You can also perform this exercise off a step – either a fitness step or a staircase. Start with your left foot on the step, making sure your heel is firmly positioned. Bring your right foot as close as you can to the step, then, as Step 1, begin to bend your knees, sitting your weight back on your right foot, so no weight goes through your left foot.

Adductor stretch

This exercise stretches the adductor muscles – the muscles that run up through your inner thigh.

1 Sit tall on either a yoga block, if you have one, or a folded towel. Open your legs to a comfortable position, allowing your knees to be slightly bent. Place your hands on the floor, in front of you close to your body. You should begin to feel a stretch in your inner thighs. For a further stretch, walk your hands further away from your body, keeping your elbows slightly bent. As you lean into the move, try to think about leaning forward from your chin with a straight back, as if you were aiming to put your chin on the floor. Release back to the start position.

HOLD FOR 10 SECONDS

KEY POINTS

If you feel uncomfortable as you stretch, try bending your legs slightly.

Hip flexor stretch

This exercise stretches the muscles in the crease at the top of the thigh – the hip flexor muscles.

1 Stand with both feet together. Take a large step back with your right leg, checking that both your feet are facing forward and that your front knee is in line over your ankle, so that you can just see your shoe laces. Drop your back knee towards the floor, until you feel the stretch in your groin area. Release back to the start position.

KEY POINTS

If you are unable to feel the stretch, try taking your back foot further away. If you feel unstable while stretching, hold the wall or a post.

HOLD FOR 10 SECONDS ON BOTH SIDES

Back stretch

1

This exercise stretches the erector spinae muscles in the lower back, helping to release any tension there.

1 Lie on your back on a mat, hug your knees into your chest, and wrap your arms around your lower legs. If you feel comfortable doing this, you may want to rock slightly from side to side as if massaging your lower back.

2 If you want to increase the stretch in Step 1, open your arms out to the side, roll your knees slowly over to the right, if possible allowing them to touch the floor. Slowly bring your knees back to the centre, relax, then take the legs over to the left side to repeat the exercise.

KEY POINTS

Keep your knees and feet together, as if holding a piece of paper between them. If your upper body feels too tight, bring your arms down to your side on the floor.

HOLD FOR 8–10 SECONDS ON BOTH SIDES

Triceps stretch

This exercise stretches the triceps – the muscles in the back of your upper arm.

1 Stand tall, with your feet about a hip-width apart. Lift your arm and reach behind your back until your right hand touches your shoulder blades (on the upper back). Try to point your right elbow up towards the ceiling. If you feel the muscles stretching in this position, then stay at this level.

2 To increase the stretch, use your left arm. Place your left hand on top of the elbow joint, and with your fingertips push your arm a little further down, allowing your right hand to slide a little further down your back. Release back to the start position.

KEY POINTS

Be careful not to push from below the elbow joint as this may cause some discomfort. Make sure that your spine stays straight, and avoid over-arching your lower back.

HOLD FOR 10 SECONDS ON BOTH SIDES

Chest stretch

This exercise stretches the pectoral muscles – the muscles in your chest.

1 Stand tall and relax your shoulders down. Open your arms out as far as it feels comfortable. Keep your elbows slightly bent as you feel the stretch across your chest.

2 If Step 1 feels easy, increase the stretch. Stand tall as before, and place your hands on the curve of your lower back. Do not push into the curve, but feel the stretch as you draw your elbows closer together.

KEY POINTS

Step 2 is a more advanced stretch, so do not attempt it if you have suffered a shoulder injury.

HOLD FOR 10 SECONDS

Your Weights Workout

Once you have completed both your general and flexibility warm-ups (see pages 20–27), you are ready to start working on the main strength section of your programme.

Once you have read through Planning your workouts (see pages 18–19), you can decide which muscle groups you are going to start with or if you wish to do the combined movements in the express workouts (see pages 82–86).

Look at each exercise first before you attempt to do it. Practise the technique of the move without any hand weights or bar (see page 14) first; when you feel comfortable with the move, choose the correct weight and start the exercise. Remember, if you feel the weight is too much or not enough, don't be afraid to stop and change it.

Also, remember not to rush the move and stop to rest immediately if you feel any discomfort or fatigue. Always perform some cool-down exercises after your workout to stretch any tight muscles and prevent injury (see page 20).

Technique is important

Learn the proper technique for each exercise before you attempt it, and always bear in mind that you need to exercise both sides of the body. If you exercise a muscle on the front of the body, make sure you do the corresponding exercise on the back.

Remember to breathe – exhale when you are exerting more energy, and inhale when the resistance is less. For example, with a biceps curl, lifting the weights to the shoulders is the more difficult phase, so this is when you breathe out. Although lowering with control back to the start position is challenging, you are working with gravity, so this is the easier phase in which to inhale, allowing your body to get enough oxygen for the muscles to work efficiently.

Move your joints through a full range of motion when doing each exercise, and perform them in a controlled manner; do not let momentum move the weights and avoid any swing movement. For example, in bicep curl, allow the bar to go all the way up to the shoulders and all the way down to the thighs.

Rest

This is an essential part of your programme – your muscles need adequate rest between each sets. If you try to work the muscles when they are fatigued, you will not achieve maximum results. A good guideline is to count slowly to about 20 between each set.

Storing results

Results of training cannot be stored, so once you stop training all the benefits you have achieved will be lost very quickly. If you have a long break from training – for example, a month or more – you may lose some of the muscle tone and strength you have achieved, and will have to begin from a lower level again. However, your body will remember some of the previous exercises and will improve faster than it would if you were starting from scratch.

Mirror, mirror

If possible always train in front of a full-length mirror to help you check that your body is maintaining a good and correct posture alignment. Continuously check in the mirror to see that both sides of your body are working together: watch that both arms lift at the same speed and to the same height, check that your back is maintaining its natural curves and that you are not slouching, rounding the shoulders, or over-arching the lower back.

Hamstrings

The hamstrings are situated on the back of the thigh. They consist of a grouping of three muscles: the bicep femoris, semimembranosus, and semitendinosus.

These muscles originate from the ischial tuberosity, which is the bottom part of the pelvis, and join the tibia and fibula (bones in the lower leg).

The hamstring muscles cross the hip and knee joint, and allow the extension and rotation of the hip and flexion at the knee.

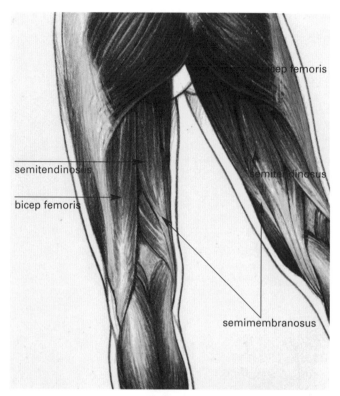

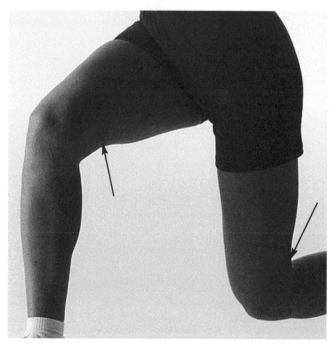

Lunge with body bar

1

2

3

This exercise is designed to work most of the major muscle groups in your thighs and buttocks, especially the hamstring muscles at the back of your thighs.

1 Start with your feet together, standing tall, and use the body bar or a pole to help keep your balance and body alignment. Take a big step back with your left leg, making sure that both your feet are facing forward and parallel. Slightly bend your left knee, and lift your heel off the floor.

2 Slowly lower your back left leg, as if you were about to kneel. Keep the bar beside your front right knee just to make sure that, as you bend your back leg, your front knee doesn't push forward over your ankle. As you look down you should always be able to see your shoe laces, then release back to the start position.

3 For a more demanding movement, use the bar to add extra resistance. Place it across the back of your shoulders, making sure it is on the soft part of the shoulders/upper back and not your neck. Hold the bar as comfortably wide as possible as you follow Steps 1 and 2 to perform the lunge.

REPEAT 10 TIMES ON BOTH SIDES X 2 SETS

KEY POINTS

Only take your back knee as far back as feels comfortable, ideally to a right angle with your ankle. You will still benefit from doing only half this movement if you start to feel discomfort in your knee. Always stand tall with a straight back.

Hamstring curl on fours

2

3

This exercise works the hamstring muscles in the back of your thighs. You will also feel other thigh muscles and the muscles in your upper body working to stabilize you in this position.

1 Kneel on a mat, and place your hands on the floor in a box position – this is where your hands are directly under your shoulders, and your knees are directly under your hips, making a box shape.

2 Lengthen your right leg out straight behind you, and slowly lift it to hip height. It is important not to lift your leg higher than this because it can encourage the hips to rotate, putting extra stress on your spine.

3 Keeping your knee in line with your hip, slowly bring your foot towards your buttocks, making sure that your upper thigh doesn't move. Return your leg to the Step 2 position, then release it back to the start position. Relax your leg down before changing sides.

REPEAT 10 TIMES ON BOTH SIDES X 2 SETS

KEY POINTS

Focus on keeping your back straight and not allowing your lower back to dip. Imagine you are balancing a tray of drinks on your back. Draw your abdominals in to support your lower spine.

Single leg stretch with ball

1

While working the hamstring muscles in this exercise you will also feel the abdominals, hip flexors and lower back working to help stabilize you in the movement.

1 Lie on your back on a mat with both knees bent. Keep your left foot flat on the floor, and place your right foot on the ball, checking that the ball is not too far away. The bent knee that is on the ball should be directly above your hip, not too close into the chest or too lengthened. Check your pelvis is in the neutral position (see page 12–13).

2 Stretch out your right leg on the ball, so that the ball slides away from you on the floor. Keep your heel on the ball and be careful not to overlengthen your leg, otherwise the ball may slide away from you. As you lengthen your leg, try to prevent your lower back arching. Check this by placing your fingertips under your lower back. If you feel it starting to arch, straighten your leg again slowly, until you can control this arching movement. Release back to the start position.

2

REPEAT 10 TIMES ON BOTH SIDES X 2 SETS

KEY POINTS

Make sure your knee stays slightly bent as you lengthen your leg. Remember to keep your shoulders relaxed, and do not not grip the mat as you perform the exercise.

Quadriceps

The quadriceps are situated at the front of the thigh. The group is made up of the following four muscles: rectus femoris, vastus medialis, vastus intermedius and vastus lateralis – hence the name quad, meaning four.

These muscles originate from the top of the pelvis and the femur (the bone in the upper thigh), then join the patella (knee joint).

The quadriceps cross over the hip and knee joints, and all the muscles help extend the knees. These muscles are particularly important in stabilizing the knee joints and ensuring correct tracking of the patella during movement.

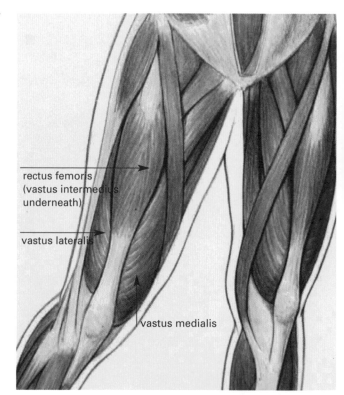

rectus femoris (vastus intermedius underneath)

vastus lateralis

vastus medialis

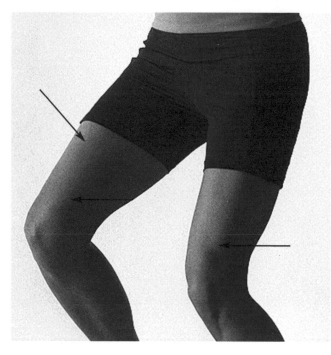

Single-leg bench squat

As well as the quadricep muscles, this exercise works the other muscles in the thighs and buttocks – the hamstrings and gluteals.

KEY POINTS

Keep your arms relaxed by your side, with your shoulders relaxed down as you perform the exercise. Only go down to a position that feels comfortable. As you progress with the move, you may find you can go a little lower, but you should never attempt to go any lower than the right angle of your knee.

REPEAT 15 TIMES ON BOTH SIDES X 2 SETS

1 Stand side on to either a fitness step or the bottom step of your staircase. Place your right foot on the step and your left foot on the floor, checking that both feet are in line with each other. The distance between the feet should be about hip-width. To increase the intensity of the exercise, hold some hand weights (see page 14) in each hand.

2 Keeping your back straight, bend your knees as if you are sitting back on an imaginary chair. Concentrate on sitting back, and not forward, so that your weight doesn't push forward over your knee joint, but works the quadriceps muscles in the front of the thigh. Release back to the start position.

Squat with body bar

2

This exercise is great for toning the muscles in the front of the thighs (quadriceps), the back of the thighs (hamstrings), and also the buttocks (gluteals). Avoid using weights in this exercise if you have knee problems.

1 Stand tall with your feet hip-width apart. Hold the body bar (see page 14) in front of you to give some initial support. To increase the intensity of the exercise, place it across the back of your shoulders.

2 Keep your back straight, and bend both knees as if sitting back on a chair. Concentrate on sitting back and not forward, so that your weight doesn't push over your knee joint, but works the quadriceps.

REPEAT 15 TIMES ON BOTH SIDES X 3 SETS

KEY POINTS

Keep the bar on the soft part of your upper back and shoulders, and not the neck. The aim of the exercise is to work the leg muscles and not to bend forward through the back. Keep your chest lifted and proud.

Leg extension with dynaband

This exercise works the quadriceps muscles in the front of the thigh. The quadriceps attach to the knee joint, so you may feel this area working, too. If you do not have a dynaband, or xertube, use a towel to add a little resistance.

1 Sit upright on the front of a dining chair – don't sit against its back. Place the dynaband (see page 14) under your right foot to begin with, making sure it is under the arch of your foot, so that it doesn't slip out. Hold the band tightly in both hands – the shorter you make the band, the harder the exercise will become.

2 Keep your knees together and extend your right leg, pulling on the dynaband, until your foot is roughly on a level with your knee. Focus on sitting tall, as your body may be tempted to tip back as you extend your leg – imagine a pole running up your back, and try not to push into the pole as you stretch your leg. Release back to the start position.

REPEAT 10 TIMES ON BOTH SIDES X 2 SETS

KEY POINTS

To begin with, you could just focus on lengthening your leg and lifting your heel. If you find it really difficult to keep your knees together, place a tennis ball between your legs to stop them moving apart.

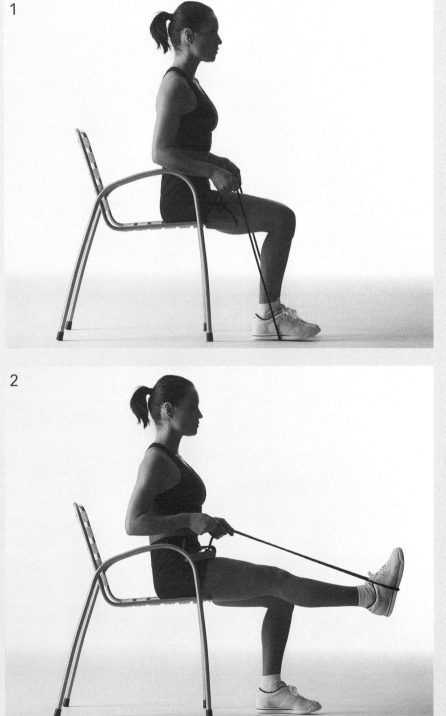

1

2

Gluteus muscles

The gluteus muscles form the buttocks. They are made up of the gluteus maximus, gluteus medius, and gluteus minimus.

The muscles originate from the sacrum and coccyx (the base of the spine) and the back of the pelvis, and join the top of the femur (the bone in the upper thigh).

They cross over the hip joint and bring about extension of the thigh, lateral rotation, and abduction of the hip (the movement when you take the leg behind and out to the side). This muscle is largely used when walking to stabilize the hip joint and prevent shuffling.

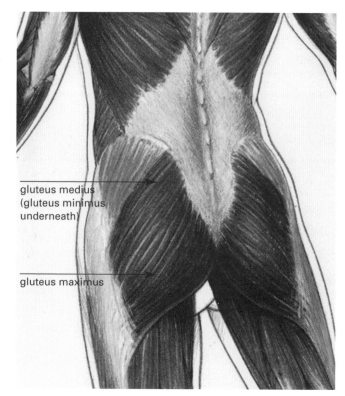

gluteus medius
(gluteus minimus
underneath)

gluteus maximus

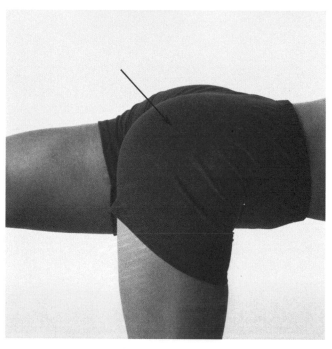

Gluteus lift

This exercise is a toning exercise for the gluteus muscle, you will also feel the muscles in the upper body and generally in the thighs working to stabilize you in this position. Performing this exercise regularly will help to shape and define this muscle group.

1 Kneel on a mat, placing your hands on the floor in a box position – this is where your hands are directly under your shoulders, and your knees under your hips, making a box shape.

2 Slowly stretch out your left leg behind you, then slowly lift your left leg to hip height. It is important not to lift the leg any higher, otherwise it will encourage your hips to rotate, putting extra stress on the spine.

3 Bend your left knee and, keeping it in line with your hip, slowly lift your heel towards the ceiling, again without rotating the hips. Take it back down just below the line of your hip, then lift again. Relax the leg down before changing to do the other side.

2

3

REPEAT 10 TIMES ON BOTH SIDES X 2 SETS

KEY POINTS

Imagine you are balancing a drink on the sole of your foot – the move you are doing is slow and quite small. Draw your lower abdominal muscles up to help support your spine, and take care that your spine doesn't dip. If you feel discomfort in your arms or shoulders, try this exercise resting on your elbows and forearms instead.

X-tuck

This exercise helps to lift the gluteus muscles – it works the muscles through a large range of movement to improve overall shape. You will also feel the muscles in the upper body and in the thighs working to stabilize you in this position.

1 Kneel on a mat, and place your hands on the floor in a box position – this is where your hands are directly under your shoulders, and your knees are directly under your hips, making a box shape. Lengthen your left leg out straight behind you and slowly lift it to hip height. It is important not to lift your leg higher than this, as it will encourage your hips to rotate, putting extra stress on the spine.

2 Bend your left knee and, keeping it in line with your hip, slowly lift your heel towards the ceiling, again without rotating your hips.

3 Drop your left knee behind your right knee, in a crossing position, then lift your heel back up towards the ceiling. Relax the leg down before changing sides.

REPEAT 10 TIMES ON BOTH SIDES X 2 SETS

KEY POINTS

Try not to sink into one side as you cross your knee behind the other, and remember to keep your back straight as if you are balancing a tray of drinks or a spirit level on your back. If you feel any discomfort in your arms or shoulders, try this exercise resting on your elbows and forearms instead.

1

2

3

Step and extend

This exercise is best done standing on a step. If you don't have a fitness step, trying using the bottom step of a staircase. Alternatively, this exercise can be done standing on the floor, but it does not give such a wide range of movement. As well as the gluteus muscles, you may also feel the muscles in your thighs working with this movement.

1

2

1 Start with your left leg placed firmly on the step. Your right leg should be parallel to your left foot, but about a foot away from the step. If you wish to increase the intensity of the exercise, add some hand weights (see page 14), but this is optional.

2 Push your weight forward onto your left leg, while drawing in your lower abdominals, and lift your right leg out behind you, lifting from the heel. Lean slightly forward to keep your spine in a straight line, like a ski slope, but do not let your lower back arch. You can either repeat the whole set on one leg or both legs alternately – alternating is harder because it requires more balance.

10 TIMES ON BOTH SIDES X 2 SETS

Calf muscles

The calf muscles comprise two major muscles called the gastrocnemius and the soleus. The gastrocnemius, with its medial and lateral heads, makes up the body of the calf situated on the back of the lower leg, and the soleus is located in the bottom part of the leg, around the ankle area.

The gastrocnemius originates from the lower part of the femur (the bone in the upper thigh), just above the knee joint, and joins the Achilles tendon, which is in the lower part of the ankle.

The soleus originates from the top of the fibula and tibia (bones in the lower leg) then also joins the Achilles tendon.

The gastrocnemius crosses the knee and ankle joint, while the soleus crosses the ankle joint. The gastrocnemius creates the flexing action of the foot (lifts the toes) and also flexes the knee, while the soleus flexes the foot.

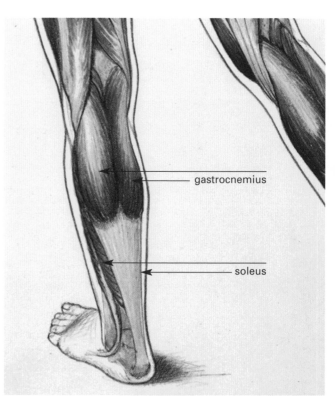

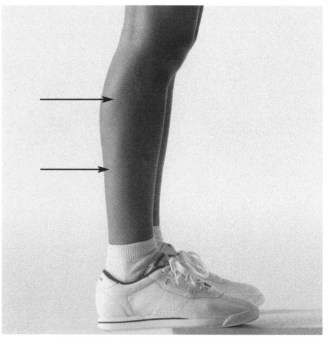

Calf raise on steps

This exercise works the calf muscles in the back of your lower leg. You may also feel the movement in other muscles of the legs as well.

1 Stand with both your feet together, and move your heels until they are off the edge of the step, so that they are hanging over it. Stand tall, with your shoulders back and your chest lifted, drawing in your abdominal muscles slightly to help you balance well.

2 Slowly lower your heels towards the floor, until you can feel your calf muscles lengthen, then bring them back up level with the step, so that you are balancing on the balls of your feet. Do this exercise slowly, but not so slowly that it becomes a stretch.

1

2

REPEAT 10 TIMES ON BOTH SIDES X 2 SETS

KEY POINTS

This exercise can be done with either a fitness step or using a step from your staircase. It is best to have a wall to hold to help you balance. The wall can either be in front of you or to the side. Alternatively, if you have good balance and wish to increase the intensity of the exercise, try using some hand weights (see page 14).

Single leg calf raise

1

2

This exercise helps to give shape and tone to the lower legs. It also helps strengthen the muscles in the lower ankle, which may be prone to injury.

1 Stand tall, holding a wall for a little support, and tuck your left foot around your right calf. Keep your chest proud and your shoulders relaxed. Lift up onto the ball of the foot, then lower your left heel back down to the floor. Release back to the start position.

2 If you find this too tricky, simply do this exercise with both feet together, lifting both heels at the same time.

REPEAT 10 TIMES ON BOTH SIDES X 2 SETS

KEY POINTS

Try not to stand too close to the wall – it is just there for support. Only touch the wall very lightly, and try not to push into the wall as you lift up.

Down dog

This is an exercise taken from the principles of yoga. Although in yoga the move is designed to work the whole body, here we are just focusing on the calf muscles in the back of your lower leg. You may also feel it in other muscles of the legs, as well as the upper body, which is being used to support you.

1 Start by kneeling on a mat and placing your hands on the floor in a box position (see Step 1 of X-tuck, page 40).

2 Slowly lengthen your legs one at a time, and try to lower your heels gently towards the floor. Soften your upper body, so that your chest folds in towards your knees, and lift your tailbone (buttocks) up to the ceiling, making a triangle shape. Then lift up onto the balls of your feet, and slowly lower your heels down again. Repeat until you have finished a set, then lower back down into the box position and rest briefly.

REPEAT 10 TIMES X 2 SETS

KEY POINTS

If you have any blood pressure problems, this exercise will not be suitable for you. Also, if at any time you feel dizzy or light-headed during this exercise, stop immediately and lower down into the box position and rest. It is great to rest in the child's pose (see page 88) between sets.

Adductors

These muscles are situated along the inner thigh. They are a thick, triangular-shaped muscle mass. The adductor group is made up of the adductor magnus (the larger part of the muscle), the adductor longus, and the adductor brevis (the small muscle attached at the top of the inner thigh).

These muscles originate from the front of the lower pelvis, mainly in the pubic area, and join the femur (the bone in the upper thigh) just above the knee joint.

The muscles cross over the hip joint and are responsible for making the leg adduct (cross over the centre line of the body, bringing the leg into the centre and past the centre line), and rotating the leg.

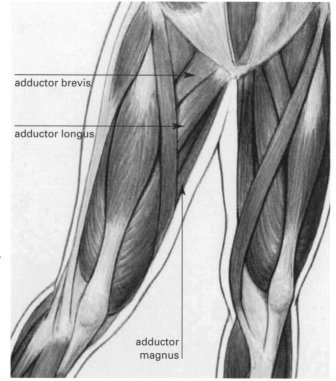

adductor brevis

adductor longus

adductor magnus

Adductor single leg lift

This exercise works the adductor muscles of the inner thigh. You may also feel it working other parts of the thighs and your upper body, which helps to stabilize you.

1 Lie on your side on your mat, then prop yourself up onto your right elbow, making sure it is not too close to your body. Lengthen your legs, and cross your top left leg over your bottom right, then place your left foot flat on the floor. Put your top left hand on the floor in front of you to stabilize you.

2 Keeping your bottom leg long, slowly begin to lift it until it touches the underneath of your top leg. Focus on keeping the bottom leg as straight as possible; although the knee will be soft, try not to let it bend. Keep your foot facing forward as you lift and lower the leg – imagine that you are balancing a cup on the inside of it. Also, when lowering your leg, try not to let your foot touch the floor until you have finished your set. Take it to just a paper width above the floor before lifting again.

3 To increase the intensity of the exercise, use a body bar (see page 14). Place one end of the bar in front of you on the floor, with the other end on the inside of your foot (always wear trainers to do this). The bar will be diagonally in front of you. Lift and lower without placing your foot on the floor until you have finished your set. Release back to the start position.

REPEAT 10 TIMES ON BOTH SIDES X 2 SETS

KEY POINTS

If you feel any discomfort in the arm that you are resting on, move it closer or further away until you find a position that reduces stress on your shoulder joint.

Drop and catch

1

2

This exercise is not only great for toning the adductor muscles of the inner thighs but also improves hand–eye coordination skills.

1 Lie on your back on your mat with both legs lifted off the floor, and place the ball between your ankles – sit up to do this if you are not very flexible. Stretch out your legs, making them a little straighter – the straighter your legs, the harder the exercise.

2 Release the ball from between your ankles and catch it on your chest, still keeping your legs in the lifted position.

3 Throw the ball up and catch it between your ankles to start the exercise again.

REPEAT 10 TIMES X 2 SETS

3

Squat and cross

This combination works the whole of the thigh and buttock area. By crossing the leg, you help to introduce the inner thigh muscle as well.

1 To help you balance, begin this exercise by holding the body bar (see page 14) in front of you with both hands. If you don't have a body bar, try using a pole. Stand tall with your feet just slightly wider than hip-width apart, keep your chest open and your shoulders relaxed.

2 Slowly move down into the squat position, as if you are going to sit down on a low chair. The squat is not the main focus of the move, so you don't need to sit too low, just enough to give you a small lift for the next part of the move.

3 As you drive up out of the squat position, keep your left leg straight as you kick it across the centre of your body (keeping to the right side of the pole) – as if you were kicking a ball across your body with the inside of your foot. Release the leg back to the start position, and begin again. You can either alternate the legs as you do the exercise or do a set on each side.

KEY POINTS

Keep your back in a neutral position (see pages 12–13), making sure that the knee that you are standing on is slightly bent, so that you do not cause stress to the knee joint.

REPEAT 10 TIMES ON BOTH SIDES X 2 SETS

Abductors

These muscles are situated on the outside of the thigh. They work jointly with the gluteus muscles to abduct the leg (take the leg out to the side).

The abductor muscles originate from the pelvic girdle, cross the hip joint, and join the femur (the bone in the upper thigh).

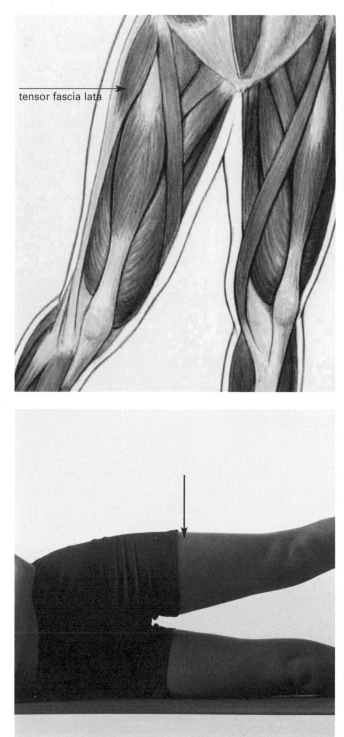

tensor fascia lata

Abductor single leg lifts

This exercise helps to tone and shape the muscles of the outer thighs and the top of the gluteus muscles.

1 Lie on your right side on a mat. Place your right hand under your head to support it. Lengthen out both legs so that they are directly on top of each other. Check that both hips, knees, and feet are stacked on top of each other, then place your left hand in front of you on the floor to help you balance.

2 Slowly lift your top (left) leg up until it is about the same height as your hips. Do not go any higher because this will cause your hips to rotate and you will be working different muscles. Slowly bring your leg back down again, without allowing it to touch your bottom leg, before repeating the lift again.

3 If you feel any discomfort or strain in your neck or upper back, lengthen your right arm along the mat and place your head down on your arm. This is actually a better position for your posture, but some people prefer to prop their head up. Try both positions and see which is more comfortable and causes the least strain as you exercise.

(continued overleaf)

KEY POINTS

Focus on keeping both hips stacked; if you feel one hip rolling forward or behind the bottom leg, you will be using other muscle groups to assist you in the move and not achieving the point of the exercise. Work through Steps 1–4 to find the best position for you. Using both legs out straight is more of a balance challenge; bending the bottom leg gives you more balance (see overleaf), but also allows you to take the top leg further down. The best position for the upper body is resting on the lower arm, but, again, see if this feels comfortable for you.

1

2

3

4 If you feel slightly unstable with both your legs straight out, try bending the underneath leg behind you, making sure you still keep both knees in line to allow the hips to stay stacked. This also allows you to work harder, because you can take the leg lower to the floor, increasing the extent of the movement.

5 If you wish to increase the challenge even further, add some resistance with the body bar (see page 14). Place one end of the bar in front of you on the floor and the other end on the centre of your foot towards the end of the bar – make sure you are wearing trainers when you do this. Simply lift and lower as before, keeping your bottom leg bent behind as in Step 4. Whichever variation you perform, don't forget to repeat the exercise on the other side.

REPEAT 10 TIMES ON BOTH SIDES X 2 SETS

4

5

Side leg with band

This exercise is similar to the single leg lift on page 51, but it has the added resistance of using the dyna band (see page 14).

1 Begin by tying a dynaband together to make a circle – make sure the knot is quite tight. Place your feet through the band until it rests above both your ankle bones, then lie on your right side on a mat. Place your right hand under your head to support it, or rest your head down on your arm. Lengthen out both legs, and make sure they are directly on top of each other. Check that both hips, knees, and feet are stacked on top of each other. Place your left hand in front of you on the floor to help you balance.

2 Slowly begin to lift your top right leg to about the same height as your hips. Do not go higher

2

because this will cause your hips to rotate and you will be working different muscles. Slowly bring the leg back down again without touching the bottom leg before lifting up again. Repeat on the other side.

REPEAT 10 TIMES ON BOTH SIDES X 2 SETS

KEY POINTS

Work within the range of the band. If your movement is very small, try a band with less resistance.

Narrow squat and lift

1   **2**   **3**

This exercise works the abductor muscles of the outer thigh. You will also feel other muscles in your thighs working, especially as this exercise brings in the squat position.

1 To balance, hold the body bar or pole (see page 14) in front of you. Stand with your feet a hip-width apart. Keep your chest open and shoulders down.

2 Slowly sit down into the squat position, as if sitting down on a low chair. As the squat is not the main focus of the move, you don't need to sit too low, just enough to give you a small lift for the next part of the move.

3 As you drive up out of the squat, with your left leg straight, allow your leg to lift out to the side. With your hips facing forward, the lift will be small but effective. Go back down to the start position. Alternate the legs or do a set on each side.

REPEAT 10 TIMES ON BOTH SIDES X 2 SETS

KEY POINTS

Focus on keeping your body in a neutral alignment, and avoid tipping over to one side. Imagine your hips have headlights and you are keeping two parallel lines of light flashing forward.

Back muscles

The back is made up of numerous muscles. The trapezius is a large, flat, triangular muscle covering most of the upper back. It is responsible for lifting the shoulder girdle.

The rhomboids assist the trapezius muscles and fix the scapula. They create that feeling of lifting the chest and sliding the shoulder down.

The latissimus dorsi is a large muscle covering most of the lower back and is responsible for adduction (bringing the arm towards the middle of the body), rotating the arm, and depressing the shoulder girdle – imagine pulling something down like a pulley: this would be the latissimus dorsi working.

And finally the erector spinae muscles run the length of the spine and are thicker in the lower spine area. They cross the vertebral column (the spine) and allow the spine to extend (lean back). These muscles are usually under-worked because we tend to spend a lot of the day in a forward flex position ie in front of a computer, in a car, in a chair etc. These muscles have an important role in maintaining stability in the spine.

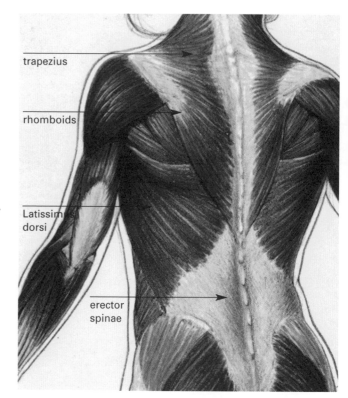

trapezius

rhomboids

Latissimus dorsi

erector spinae

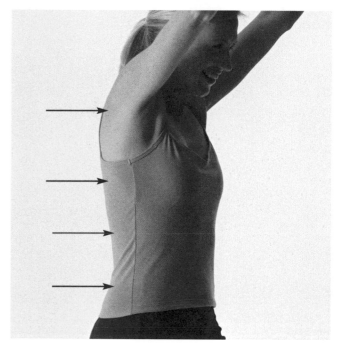

Seated row with dynaband

This exercise works the latissimus dorsi, the large muscle in the back. It is a great strength exercise helping to reduce back pain and improve posture.

1 Sit tall on a mat with your knees bent. Hook the dynaband around the soles of your feet, making sure that the band is in the middle of the foot, not too close to your toes as it may come off, which could be dangerous. Lengthen your legs out in front of you, but still keep your knees slightly bent. Hold on to the band handles, keeping your arms relaxed.

2 Begin to draw the handles in towards your body, keeping your elbows tucked in close, so that you feel your shoulder blades sliding in together, then slowly allow your hands to slide forward back into the start position. Do the movement back and forth to a four-second count.

REPEAT 10 TIMES X 2 SETS

KEY POINTS

The straighter your legs, the more tension you will create on the band and the harder the exercise will become. However, you need to keep your knees slightly soft to avoid locking out and causing stress to the knee joint.

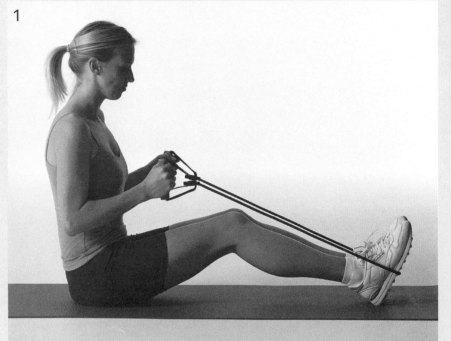

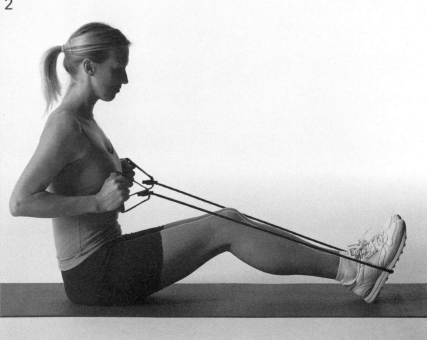

One-arm row

2

This exercise works the deltoids (see page 58) and latissimus dorsi – the muscles in the shoulder and back area. You will also feel the muscles in the arms working, although they are not the focus.

1 Kneel on a mat, and place your left arm on a stool, bench, or low chair. Make sure you can rest on it without sinking into your shoulder. If it is too high it can cause stress and tension in your shoulder. Take a hand weight (see page 14) in your right hand and lean slightly forward into the stool, keeping your back straight and flat.

2 Keeping the rest of your body still, lift your right arm up as if you are trying to start a petrol lawn mower. As you draw the arm up, keep it close to your body with your elbow tucked in. Keep drawing the arm up until you feel your shoulder blades sliding together, then slowly lower your arm down towards the floor until it is nearly straight, but do not touch the floor. Try to go up and down to a four-second count.

REPEAT 10 TIMES ON BOTH SIDES X 2 SETS

KEY POINTS

Draw your abdominal muscles in to help support your back as you do the exercise. Imagine that you are balancing something on your back so that you do not move your torso, but only your arm.

Military press

1

2

3

This exercise works the trapezius, the deltoids (see page 58) and the triceps – the muscles in the upper back, the shoulders, and the arms. It is a great exercise for the upper body, but do it slowly if you have blood pressure problems.

1 Stand with your feet in the lunge position, with one foot forward and one back. Keep your feet parallel and your knees slightly bent. This is a good position if you have any discomfort in your lower back area or have trouble maintaining a neutral alignment, and as you do the exercise with heavier weights. Raise your hand weights (see page 14) until they are level with your ears in the start position. Keep your palms facing forward and not into your body.

2 Slowly lift your arms up towards the ceiling, extending them until your arms are nearly straight, but your elbows are slightly bent, to prevent putting excessive strain on the elbow joint. Take the weights back down to the start position just above the shoulders. Focus on keeping your elbows out from the body as you perform the exercise, and maintain a tall, neutral alignment of the body, especially the spine. Keep the movements slow and controlled and try to make each phase of the move last for four to five seconds.

3 If you can maintain good neutral posture, you can perform this exercise standing tall, with your feet about a hip-width apart.

REPEAT 10 TIMES X 2 SETS

KEY POINTS

Draw in your abdominal muscles to help support your spine and maintain a neutral alignment.

Shoulders

There are three muscles that make up the shoulder pad. They are grouped as the deltoid muscles, but are separately called the deltoid anterior, medial and posterior, and each part of the deltoid has a slightly different function.

The muscles originate from the clavicle area (collar bone) then join the top of the humerus (the bone in the top of the arm).

The anterior (front) muscle makes a flexing action, taking the arm up in front and rotating it. The medial (middle) muscle abducts the arm, taking it away from the body, and the posterior (behind or back) muscle extends the arm, lifts it behind, and rotates it. These muscles are essential for stabilizing the shoulder joint.

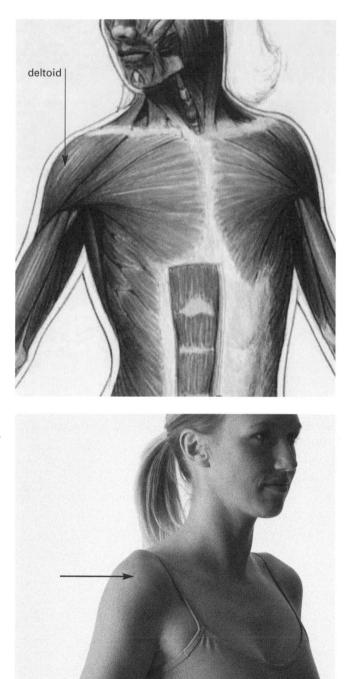

deltoid

Reverse fly

1

2

A good general exercise for the shoulder and upper-arm area, this exercise also works the latissimus dorsi – the large muscles in the back.

1 Sit on a chair or bench, making sure that the chair isn't too high and that your knees are in line with your hips – not too high or low. Move forward so that your chest is on your legs, holding the hand weights (see page 14) together under your legs.

2 Keeping your chest on your thighs, slowly begin to lift up the weights, opening your arms out to the side. Keep your elbows slightly bent, so that you feel your shoulder blades squeezing together. Imagine your arms are flying, but keep the move slow and controlled as you move them in and out to a four-second count.

REPEAT 10 TIMES X 2 SETS

KEY POINTS

Keep your head relaxed, and don't lift it up as you lift your arms. Your chest should remain on your thighs until you have completed your set. Finally, make sure that your feet are far enough away from the chair that the hand weights can meet each other under your legs every time.

Frontal raise

This exercise works the anterior, deltoid, and pectoralis major muscles – the muscles in the front of the shoulders, the shoulders, and the chest.

1 Stand tall, with your hand weights (see page 14) held each side of your body. Start with your feet together; however, if you feel slightly unstable, stand with them about hip-width apart.

2 Slowly raise your left arm up in front of you, until it is about level with your shoulder, then slowly bring it down again. Try to lift and lower the weight to a slow count of about four to five seconds each way.

3 If you want to increase the resistance of the exercise or decrease your workout time, lift both weights at the same time, concentrating on maintaining a tall, neutral position.

REPEAT 10 TIMES ON BOTH SIDES X 2 SETS

Lateral raise

1

2

This exercise works the lateral or medial deltoid – the muscles on the side of the shoulders.

1 Stand tall, holding your hand weights (see page 14) together at about navel height, with your elbows slightly bent. Start with your feet together; however, if you feel slightly unstable, stand with them about hip-width apart.

2 Slowly take your arms out to the side, until they reach shoulder height, then slowly return them back down to the start position. Allow the weights to come very close together, but do not let them touch. Try to lift and lower to a slow count of about four to five seconds each way.

REPEAT 10 TIMES X 2 SETS

Triceps

The full name of this muscle is the triceps brachii. This muscle has three heads, and it covers the whole of the back of the upper arm.

The long head of this muscle originates from the scapula (the shoulder blade) just above the shoulder joint. The other two heads originate from the humerus (the bone in the top of the arm) and the muscle, then inserts into the ulna (the bone in the lower arm).

The muscles cross the shoulder and elbow joints and are responsible for extension of the elbows and shoulders, and also assist in shoulder stabilization and adduction.

This part of the body is usually a problem area for most women because it tends to attract fat stores, and is generally under-used in comparison to the bicep muscles.

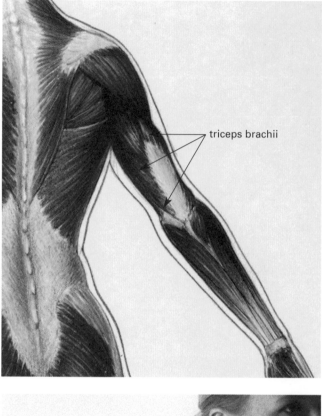

triceps brachii

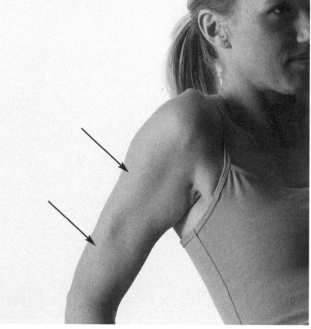

Push-up

This exercise works the major pectoral muscles in the chest, but you will also be working the triceps and the shoulders.

1 Kneel on a mat, and place your hands on the floor in a box position – this is where your hands are directly under your shoulders and your knees under your hips, making a box shape. Practise this move side on to a mirror to begin with so that you can check your body alignment. This is the first stage of the push-up. Now imagine a line running between your hands on the mat, and aim to touch your nose right down on the line. Initially you may not be able to go right down to the floor, but with practice this should be possible. In the meantime, go as low as you can, so that your body feels the pressure but you stay in control of the overall movement. Try to go up and down to a four-second count.

2 As this exercise becomes easier, it is important to challenge your body further to keep achieving results. Walk your hands further forward this time, then cross your ankles and tip your weight forward so that again your nose is over that imaginary line. For the maximum challenge, try to perform a few of these push-ups with your legs straight. As soon as you feel you are letting your back sink, stop and continue the push-ups on the lower level.

3 The final challenge is to perform the push-up with your legs straight – this is a lot harder to do as your upper body has to work more to lift your body weight. Try to do this exercise with a mirror by you, so that you can check that your spine stays in a neutral alignment. As soon as you see or feel that your lower back is sinking, or increasing its natural curve, rest down, or try a lower level.

REPEAT 15 TIMES X 2 SETS

KEY POINTS

Find a level at which you can perform the exercise for at least 15 repetitions without losing posture alignment. You need to challenge your body, but with control and without risking injury.

Triceps extension

This exercise works the triceps in the back of the arm. It is best done on a fitness step or bench (see page 14); however, it can also be done on a mat. The easier level uses hand weights; the harder level uses a body bar.

1 Start by lying on your back on the step (see page 14); with your knees bent and your feet flat on the floor. Hold the hand weights (see page 14) in your hands, and lift up your arms to the ceiling, making sure that your hands are over your shoulders. Relax your shoulders and soften your elbows to prevent stress in these two areas.

2 Keeping your elbows directly above your shoulders, begin to lower your hands behind you until the weights are either side of your head, close to your ears. Check that the upper part of your arms do not move – the movement is from the elbow to hand only. Also keep your elbows parallel to each other to avoid them falling open. Lift the weights up and down to a four-second count.

3 For a more advanced level, use a body bar (see page 14). Start as Step 1, holding the bar up towards the ceiling with your arms straight. The distance between your hands should be about the same distance as two hands – 20cm (8in) apart.

4 Slowly lower the bar towards your forehead, until it is about 2.5cm (1in) above it. Keep your elbows parallel to each other, as above, as you lift up and down to a four-second count. Imagine that you are pointing your elbows towards the ceiling.

REPEAT 10 TIMES X 2 SETS

1

2

KEY POINTS

If you feel any discomfort in your elbow joint, stop completely or switch to a lighter weight. Keep your spine in a neutral position, so that it does not curve more as you perform the exercise. If you are lying on a bench, place your feet at the edge of it.

Triceps dip

1

2

3

This exercise works the triceps muscles, but you will also feel muscles in the shoulders and torso working. The exercise can be performed on a number of pieces of equipment/furniture such as a chair, sofa, fitness step (see page 14), or the bottom step of a staircase.

1 Using a chair, place your hands on the edge of the chair (make sure the chair is stable and not likely to topple or slide from under you). Point your fingertips towards your buttocks, keeping the ball of your hands firmly on the chair. Bend your knees, keeping your feet flat on the floor in front of the chair, while your buttocks hover in mid air.

2 Slowly bend your elbows, lowering your buttocks towards the floor, then up back to the start position to a count of four seconds. In the start position, try to imagine that you are balancing a tray of drinks on your thighs.

3 If you wish to increase the intensity of the exercise, do a one-leg triceps dip, which is shown here on a fitness step, but can be performed on a chair. Start as Step 1, and cross your right leg over your left, resting your ankle just above your knee joint and perform the exercise as above. Try not to bring your left foot too close to your buttocks because this may stress the knee joint.

REPEAT 10 TIMES X 2 SETS

KEY POINTS

To increase the challenge in either level, simply move your feet a little further away from your buttocks. If you feel a lot of tension in your shoulders, bring your hands closer to your buttocks. You may feel some discomfort in your wrists, so rest between sets and shake them.

Biceps

These muscles are situated in the front of the arm. The major bicep is called the bicep brachii and originates from the top of the scapula (the shoulder blade) and joins the radius (the bone in the lower arm), crossing over the elbow joint and the shoulder. This muscle is responsible for flexing the elbow joint, bringing the hand towards the shoulder, and supporting the shoulder when the arm is held out straight.

The brachialis originates from the lower part of the humerus (the bone in the top of the arm) and joins the ulna (the other bone in the lower arm). This muscle is normally the first one to work at the start of a move (see bicep curls, pages 67–69).

The brachioradialis also originates in the lower part of the humerus and joins the lower part of the radius, close to the wrist. The brachialis and the brachioradialis help to flex the elbow.

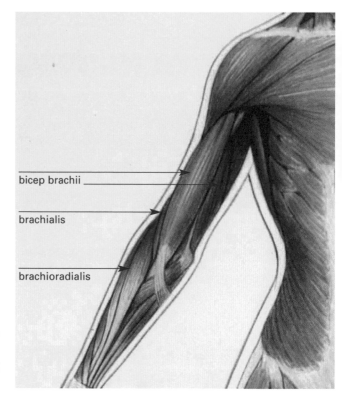

bicep brachii

brachialis

brachioradialis

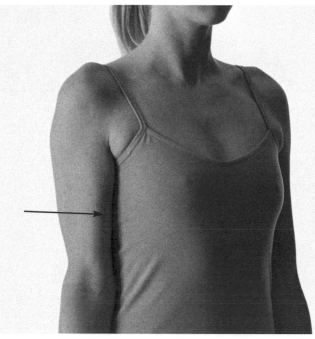

Concentrate curl

This exercise works the biceps muscles in the front of the arms. It can be performed sitting on a chair, a sofa, a fitness step (see page 14), or a gym bench.

1 Sit on the front of the chair with your legs slightly more than a hip-width apart. Place your right hand on your right thigh to stabilize your upper body position. Allow your left arm holding a hand weight (see page 14) to lengthen between your legs, placing your elbow on the inside of your knee. As you lean forward, try not to hunch over your legs, keeping your back straight and long, imagining it is a ski slope.

2 Keeping your elbow tucked against the inside of your knee, slowly lift the weight towards your left shoulder to a count of four seconds, then slowly return it down to the start position. Keep the move slow and controlled, so that you do not allow the weight to drop down too quickly to the start position.

REPEAT 10 TIMES X 2 SETS

KEY POINTS

This exercise is called 'concentrate curl' because its purpose is to concentrate all the effort into the biceps muscle only. As you perform it, focus on keeping the rest of your body still and braced, especially your lower abdominals and spine. If you feel that you are slouching, you may need to use a tall chair. It can be hard to maintain good posture if you do this exercise on a low stool or fitness step.

1

2

Standing curl

This exercise works the biceps muscles in the front of the arms. It can be done with either hand weights or handmade options (see page 14). Here a dynaband is used (see page 14).

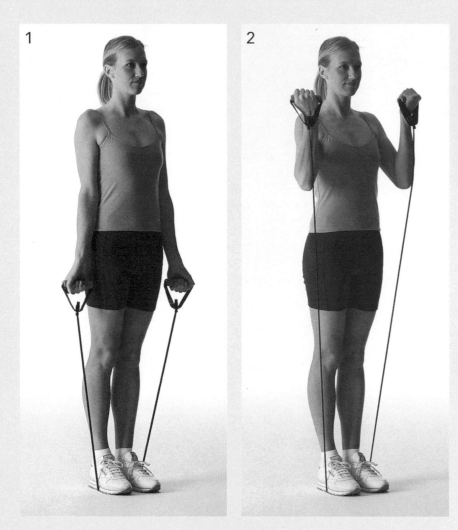

1

2

KEY POINTS

The further apart your feet are, the more resistance there will be on the band because it will be shortened. If you find the band too challenging, either change to a lower-level band or bring your feet a little closer.

1 Stand tall, and put the dynaband under your feet, holding the handles firmly in each hand. Stand tall with your arms by your side, your elbows tucked in, and your palms facing forward.

2 Slowly lift up your hands to your shoulders then lower them again. Do this exercise in a four-second lift and lower sequence with your elbows close to your sides for momentum.

REPEAT 10 TIMES X 2 SETS

Hammer curl

As well as the biceps muscles, you will also feel the muscles in the forearm working in this exercise.

1 Stand tall with your feet about a hip-width apart, holding your hand weights (see page 14) at your side, with your palms facing inward. Tuck your elbows into your waist.

2 Keeping your elbows tucked in, slowly lift the weights towards your shoulders, then move them slowly back down again to the start position. Try to do this exercise in a steady four-second lift and lower sequence.

REPEAT 10 TIMES X 2 SETS

KEY POINTS

Try to keep your shoulders relaxed, maintaining a long distance between your shoulders and your ears. Draw in your lower abdominals slightly to help you maintain a tall, neutral alignment.

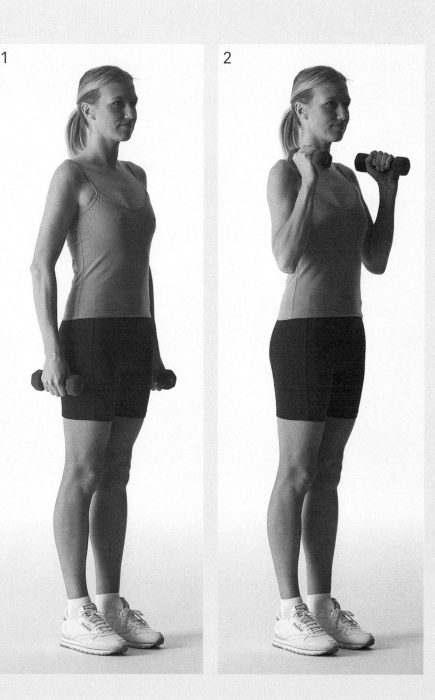

1

2

Chest muscles

The muscles of the chest are the pectoralis major and minor. These muscles lie under the breasts and are generally responsible for the shape of the breast, ie whether they are firm or low-slung. The major muscle originates from the clavicle (the collar bone) and the sternum (the bone that runs down through the centre of the chest and the ribs), then joins the humerus (the bone in the top of the arm).

The pectoralis minor muscle originates from the rib cage and joins the scapula. Both muscles are responsible for adducting and rotating the arm, and bringing the arm across the chest. The pectoralis muscle also rotates the shoulder joint and is responsible for depressing the scapula (the shoulder blade).

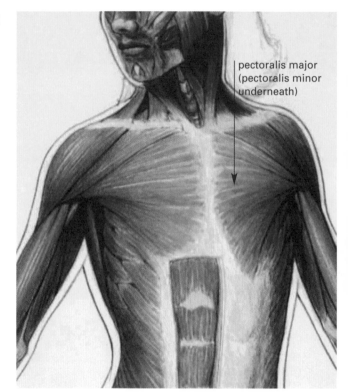

pectoralis major (pectoralis minor underneath)

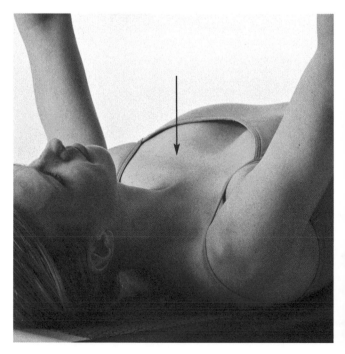

Fly – flat

As well as the pectoralis major muscle, you will feel the biceps and triceps muscles stabilizing the movement, and the deltoids assisting it. This exercise is best done on a fitness step or bench (see page 14); however, it can also be done simply on a mat on the floor.

1 Lie on your back on your step with your knees bent and your feet flat. Hold the hand weights (see page 14) in each hand, and lift up your arms to the ceiling. Try to make sure that your hands are directly above your shoulders and not over your head or your chest. Relax your shoulders slightly, and soften your elbows to prevent any stress occurring in these two areas.

2 Open your arms, slowly lowering them towards the floor. Keep your elbows slightly bent to avoid placing any stress on your elbow joints. Once your hands are just below the level of your shoulders (or just above the floor if you are lying on the floor only), bring the weights back up to the start position, with your arms nearly straight but your elbows soft. Try to do this exercise in a steady four-second lift and lower sequence.

REPEAT 10 TIMES X 2 SETS

KEY POINTS

If you feel any discomfort in your lower back, try placing your feet on a small block, such as a telephone directory.

Flys – incline

The fitness step or bench (see page 14) is set on an incline to do this great version of the fly. The benefit of this exercise is that the focus is on the top part of the pectoralis major, which helps to fight the forces of gravity and keep the chest firm and lifted.

1 Set the fitness step or bench in an incline position. With a fitness step, simply change the positions of the risers; a fitness bench normally comes with adjustments. The aim is to have the head end of the step/bench higher than the hip end. Follow Steps 1 and 2 in the flys –flat exercise above, lifting and lowering the weights in a smooth, four-second sequence.

REPEAT 10 TIMES X 2 SETS

KEY POINTS

Keep the speed of the movement slow in this exercise. Do not allow your arms to go too low because this may strain your muscles and shoulder joint. Keep your spine in a neutral position on the step – be aware of trying not to increase the curve in your lower back as you perform the exercise.

Body-bar press

This exercise primarily works the pectoralis major muscle in the chest and also the triceps muscles in the back of your arms. You may also feel the deltoid muscles in your shoulders working. It can be performed on a fitness step, a bench (see page 14), or simply on the floor.

KEY POINTS

Try to keep your shoulders relaxed and down as you do the exercise. If you don't have a body bar or weights bar, perform this exercise with your hand weights (see page 14).

1 Start lying on your back on your step, with your knees bent and your feet flat – keep them comfortably close to your buttocks. Hold the body bar (see page 14) just wider than shoulder-width with an over-grip, and rest the bar just above the middle of your chest.

2 Slowly take your arms up to the ceiling. When your arms are straight, with your elbows slightly bent to avoid stressing the elbow joint, slowly lower the bar back to the start position. As you take the bar to the ceiling, keep it above the centre of your chest. Try to do this exercise in a four-second lift and lower sequence.

REPEAT 10 TIMES X 2 SETS

Pec deck

1

2

This exercise works the pectoralis major muscle in the chest. You will also feel the biceps, triceps, and deltoids in the arms and shoulders working. This exercise is best done seated on a chair, bench, or sofa. You can also do it standing; however, it is harder to maintain a neutral spine alignment doing it this way.

1 Sit tall in a neutral alignment on the edge of the seat of a chair, with your feet close to it. Holding your hand weights (see page 14), lift your arms up until your elbows are in line with your shoulders, then slowly close your elbows together, keeping your hands at a right angle to your elbows.

2 Keeping your elbows up in line with your shoulders, open your arms out until you can no longer see your elbows out of the corner of your eyes. At this stage you should also feel the muscles in the chest working; now bring your arms back to the start position. Try to do this exercise in a four-second open and close sequence.

REPEAT 10 TIMES X 2 SETS

KEY POINTS

Imagine you are sitting against a hard chair – this will help you to sit up tall and prevent you stressing your back muscles. If you feel any discomfort in your lower back, do the exercise on a chair with a high back that allows you to sit up straight with a little support, but do not push into the back of the chair.

Abdominals

The two main abdominal muscles are the
rectus abdominus and the deeper muscles, the
transversus abdominus.

The rectus abdominus ('six-pack muscle')
originates from the front of the pelvis, runs
the length of the torso, and joins the middle
of the rib cage and sternum. It is responsible
for forward flexion (bending forward) and
rotation of the vertebral column, and also
stabilizes the pelvis during walking. It is
the prime mover in exercises such as sit-ups
(see page 75).

The transversus abdominus is a deeper
muscle lying under the rectus muscle. The
transversus muscle supports the abdominal
organs and stabilizes the torso, assisting good
posture and neutral alignment. This muscle
is not activated in general exercise where
weights are used, such as most of those in this
book. To activate this muscle, imagine you are
wearing a wide belt and, as this tightens, you
feel the sensation of the abdominal area
drawing in (static contractions) – this is the
transversus muscle working.

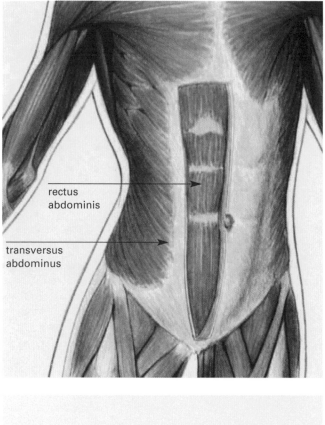

rectus
abdominis

transversus
abdominus

Basic crunch

1

2

This exercise strengthens the large rectus abdominus muscles in the stomach. You may also feel the erector spinae muscles in the back working and the muscles in the hip flexors as well.

1 Lie on your mat on the floor with your knees bent and feet flat, and find the natural curve of the lumbar spine (see page 12–13). Take your hands to the back of your head to act as a cradle for the weight of your head. Be careful not to use them to pull the head up because this will cause discomfort and strain your neck and shoulders. Open your elbows out wide so that you can't see them out of the corner of your eyes.

2 Slowly lift your head and shoulders a few inches off the floor. Focus on drawing your lower abdominals down slightly, so they don't rise into a dome; this will happen a bit, but avoid it as much as possible. Keep your elbows wide and point your chin slightly towards your chest. Slowly lower yourself down again without quite touching the floor, then lift up again – keep a paper width between your shoulders and the floor until you have finished the set. Try to do this exercise in a four-second lift and lower sequence. With practice, you can probably raise your shoulders a little further off the floor, but do not go too high – the middle of your back should stay on the floor at all times.

REPEAT 10 TIMES X 2 SETS

KEY POINTS

If you find this exercise difficult or uncomfortable with your arms in this position, fold them across your body or have them sliding up your thighs as you lift. To begin with you may feel some tension in your neck and shoulders. This may be because your neck is not used to holding your head in this position. If you lift from the head like a nodding dog, this will just increase the tension, so focus on keeping your head still, allowing your arms to carry some of the weight to begin with.

Reverse curl

1

2

3

4

This exercise works a variety of muscles in the torso, mainly the rectus abdominus and the erector spinae muscles in the back.

1 Lie on the floor on your mat with your knees bent and your feet flat. Find the natural curve of the lower spine (see pages 12–13). Place your hands by your side on the floor, palms down. Slowly lift one foot off the floor, then the other, keeping your knees bent. Intertwine your feet with one ankle on top of the other. Try to keep your spine in a neutral position.

2 Imagine that a rope from the ceiling is tied around your ankles. As the rope is pulled up, draw in your lower abdominals, moving your pubic bone very slowly towards your chest as your hips lift off the floor. Try to focus on your lower abdominals lifting your lower body and not the hip flexors, then relax back down to the start position.

3 The more you straighten your legs, the harder the move becomes. When your legs are practically straight, you can feel the move becoming more of an upward lift.

4 Try not to push into the floor with your hands too much. As you become stronger and more confident with this move, turn your hands, palms up, so they don't assist with the move, or cross your arms over your chest.

REPEAT 10 TIMES X 2 SETS

KEY POINTS

If you are simply rocking your legs over your chest, like a ball, this is not really working the back muscles that you should be focusing on. To begin with, aim for a small and subtle but effective movement – don't worry if you are only able to lift the tailbone a few inches off the floor. Take a rest if you feel any discomfort in your lower back.

Plank

This exercise works all the muscles in your torso – this includes the deeper abdominal muscles called the transversus abdominus, the muscles of the spine, and also the muscles that support the shoulder girdle – the trapezius, deltoid, and latissimus dorsi.

1

2

1 Lie flat on your stomach on your mat or a soft surface, with your feet relaxed out behind you, toes facing downwards. Bring your elbows in under your shoulders, and lift your shoulders off the floor, then your chest and stomach, and finally your hips – if you looked in a mirror, your back should be long and smooth like a ski slope. Hold this position and breathe normally, then release back down to the start position. If your lower back sinks or you have any discomfort, stop and rest.

2 To challenge yourself further, try this exercise keeping your legs straight. This will make your torso work harder because it has more weight to maintain in this posture. From the Step 1 position, push up and slowly lengthen each leg out, one at time, until both legs are out straight. Try not to push your buttocks up, creating a pyramid shape. Your hips should stay in line with your shoulders, without allowing your lower back to sink. If you feel it sinking, lower and relax.

KEY POINTS

Try not to crunch your shoulders up around your ears while doing the movement. As you lift up, imagine a tall candle burning under your stomach. Lift your stomach higher to avoid it being burnt by the candle.

TRY TO HOLD FOR 10 SLOW BREATHS
REPEAT 10 TIMES X 2 SETS

Obliques

The obliques, the muscles around the waist, are comprised of two muscles: the external obliques and the internal obliques.

The external obliques are a broad band of muscle on each side of the trunk, which originates from the lower eight ribs and joins the linea alba going into the pelvic area. The external obliques work when the vertebral column is flexed, leaning forward, and when rotation and lateral flexion are performed together: imagine standing tall and reaching your right hand down your thigh towards your knee – this is lateral flexion.

The internal obliques originate from the lumbar fascia and front of the pelvis and join the linea alba and the bottom three ribs. They also work when the spine is flexed, rotated, and laterally flexed.

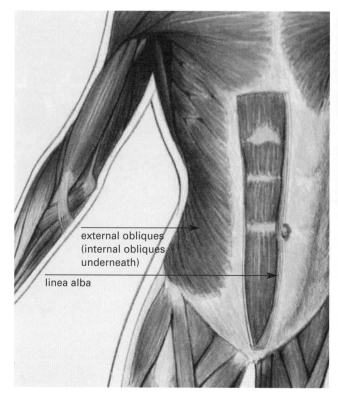

external obliques
(internal obliques
underneath)

linea alba

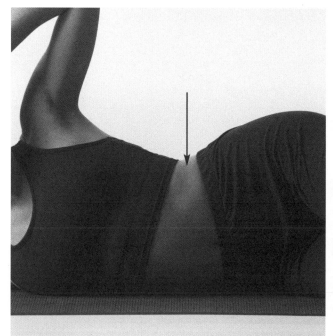

Crunch twist

This exercise works the muscles around the waistline, primarily the oblique muscles. You may also feel the muscles in the back and hip flexors working slightly.

1 Lie on the floor with your knees bent and feet flat on the mat, and find the natural curve of your lower spine (see page 12–13). Put your hands behind your head to act as a cradle for the weight of your head, but do not use them to pull your head up, as this will cause discomfort and strain in your neck and shoulders. Open your elbows out wide, so that you can't see your elbows when you look out of the corner of your eyes.

2 Slowly begin to lift your head and shoulders a few inches off the floor. Focus on drawing your lower abdominals down slightly, so they don't rise into a dome; this will happen a bit, but avoid it as much as possible. As you lift up, reach with your left hand across your body to the outside of your right knee. Slowly lower again without quite touching the floor, before lifting up again, keeping a paper-width space between your shoulders and the floor, until you have finished the set.

REPEAT 10 TIMES X 2 SETS

KEY POINTS

The further you reach, the harder the exercise is. So to begin with, just focus on reaching towards your knee, then progress to reaching for the knee. Think about creating a diagonal fold across your abdominals.

1

2

Hip stacked lift

KEY POINTS

Don't fling your head and shoulders upwards, or let your torso pull forward. Remember that the correct muscle contraction, not the movement of the upper torso, is important.

This exercise works the muscles in the waistline, the obliques, and the quadratus lumborum in the lower back.

1 Lie on your right side on your mat with both legs bent and your knees, hips, and ankles stacked (for a full range of motion, place a rolled towel or small pillow under your waist). Place both hands behind your head, with your right arm resting on the floor. Your left elbow should be pointing up towards the ceiling.

2 Slowly lift your rib cage towards the top of your hip – focus on contracting the lateral muscles between your ribs and your hipbones – then release back to the start position. If you can't lift yourself at first, don't worry – it does take a little practice.

REPEAT 15 TIMES ON BOTH SIDES X 2 SETS

Cycle

1

2

KEY POINTS

The higher you stretch out your legs, the easier the exercise becomes, especially on your lower back. If you wish to challenge your self further with this exercise, try taking your legs lower towards the floor. If you feel any discomfort in your lower back, stop and rest briefly, and only continue the move if the pain does not return.

This exercise works all the muscles in your torso area, including the back muscles – you will feel this movement in your rectus abdominus, your obliques, and lower back. If you feel any discomfort in your lower back during exercise, stop. Only restart if the discomfort does not continue.

1 Lie on your mat with your knees bent and your feet flat, and find the natural curve of your lower spine (see page 12–13). Place your hands behind your head. Open your elbows out wide so that you can't see them out of the corner of your eyes.

2 Slowly lift one foot off the floor, then the other, and then your shoulders, like a concertina. Stretch your legs away from you alternately in a pumping motion, taking your opposite elbow to the knee that is closest to your chest – for example, take your right elbow to your left knee as it comes in to your chest. Keep alternating the legs and arms in a smooth movement as if you were cycling to a four-second lift and lower sequence. After doing a set of this exercise, slowly lower one leg, then the other to prevent putting any strain on your lower back.

REPEAT
10 TIMES X 2 SETS

Express workouts

This selection of moves has been put together to allow you to work several parts of the body at once. It is a great workout if you are short of time and would like to train your whole body in one go. However, performing combined moves does take more control and effort, so they are not always ideal for beginners.

When performing each exercise, focus on the quality of each part of the move, for example, the leg lift and the arm extension. If you have worked through the rest of this book, you should have a good understanding of the best techniques and postures, so apply these in the moves as well.

The express 40-minute workout programme can be done as an additional day to your programme, or you can repeat this whole programme twice a week. Once you have worked through all the moves, performing the stated number of reps and sets (which should take you about 40 minutes), you should finish with a cool down and stretch. If you are short of time, you could use some of the moves as a gentle warm-up, Start with the beginner moves, using light or no weights, then repeat them with more weights, increasing the level of difficulty.

Express 40-minute workout, once a week

LEVEL	MAJOR MUSCLE	EXERCISE	PAGE	REPS	SETS
Beg	Legs and upper body	Squat with a kick and press	83	10 each leg	1
Beg	Legs and upper body	Squat, lift, and row	84	10 each leg	1
Beg	Legs and arms	Lunge and curl	85	10	1
Beg	Total body	Clean and press	86	10	1
Beg	Abdominals	Basic crunch	75	10	1
Beg	Obliques	Crunch twist	79	10	1
Int	Legs and upper body	Squat with a kick and press	83	12 each leg	2
Int	Legs and upper body	Squat, lift, and row	84	12 each leg	2
Int	Legs and arms	Lunge and curl	85	12	2
Int	Total body	Clean and press	86	12	2
Int	Abdominals	Reverse curl	76	12	2
Int	Obliques	Hip stacked lift	80	12	2
Adv	Legs and upper body	Squat with a kick and press	83	15 each leg	3
Adv	Legs and upper body	Squat, lift, and row	84	15 each leg	3
Adv	Legs and arms	Lunge and curl	85	15	3
Adv	Total body	Clean and press	86	15	3
Adv	Abdominals	Plank	77	10	2
Adv	Obliques	Cycle	81	15	3

Squat with a kick and press

This exercise is best done on a fitness step (see page 14) or the bottom step of a staircase, or you could do it simply standing on the floor. It works the muscles of the thighs (the quadriceps, hamstrings, and gluteus), the hip flexors, and the muscles in the upper body (the trapezes, deltoids, triceps and latissimus dorsi).

1 Start side on to the step, with your right foot on the step and your left foot on the floor. Keep both feet about hip-width apart. Lift up your hand weights (see page 14) to shoulder height. Stand tall, and slightly draw in your abdominal muscles.

2 Sit down into the squat position – imagine you are sitting down on an invisible seat, and focus on sitting slightly back rather than forward to avoid putting any strain on your knees. Keep your weights at shoulder height.

3 As you drive up out of the squat position, lift your left leg forward from the hip socket, as if you are kicking a soft ball away from you. As you extend your leg, also extend the weights towards the ceiling, keeping your elbows slightly bent. Slowly lower your leg back down to the squat position and bring the weights back down to the start position to begin the exercise again. This should be done in one long, continuous movement.

REPEAT 15 TIMES ON BOTH SIDES X 2 SETS, OR ALTERNATIVELY WORK ON ALTERNATE SIDES

Squat, lift, and row

This exercise is also best done on a fitness step (see page 14) or the bottom step of a staircase, or by simply standing on the floor. It will work the muscle of the thighs – the quadriceps, hamstrings, gluteus, and abductors – along with muscles in the upper body – the trapezes, deltoids, triceps, and latissimus dorsi.

1 Start side on to the step, with your right foot on the step and your left foot on the floor. Keep your feet about hip-width apart. Hold your hand weights (see page 14) in front of you, just below your navel. The weights should be touching and horizontal. Stand tall, and slightly draw in your abdominal muscles.

2 Start to squat down – imagine you are sitting down on an invisible seat, and focus on sitting slightly back rather than forward, to avoid putting any strain on your knees. Keep the weights in front of you at navel height.

3 As you drive up out of the squat position, lift your left leg out to the side, being careful not to rotate or tip your hips as you do this. Keep both hips facing forward and almost level. At the same time, draw your weights up your body to about collarbone height, keeping your elbows out wide, then slowly lower them back down to the start position, while returning your leg to the squat position. Perform the exercise in a smooth, continuous movement.

REPEAT 15 TIMES ON BOTH SIDES X 2 SETS, OR WORK ON ALTERNATE SIDES

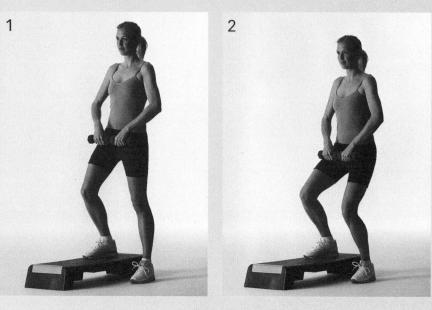

Lunge and curl

This exercise will work the muscles in the thighs – the quadriceps, hamstrings, and gluteus – the hip flexors, and the muscles in the upper body – the trapezes, deltoids, biceps, triceps and latissimus dorsi.

1 Start with both feet together, holding your hand weights (see page 14) beside your legs. Stand tall, with your chest lifted and draw in your abdominal muscles slightly.

2 Step your left leg forward into the lunge position with both your feet facing forward, keeping the heel of the back leg slightly lifted. Try to practise this exercise side on to a mirror so that you can check that your posture is correct throughout the move. Hold your weights down beside the top of your legs at this stage of the exercise.

3 Slowly lower your back leg, pointing the back knee towards the floor. Check in the mirror that the front leg is not pushing over your front knee – looking down your front knee, you should still see your shoe laces. If you cannot, then step further forward. As you lower your back knee, bring your weights up to shoulder height. Keep your elbows tucked in as you slowly drive up into the lunge position again, then lower your weights back down by your side. Step your feet together so you are back at the start position. All stages of the exercise should link together as one long, smooth movement.

REPEAT 15 TIMES ON BOTH SIDES X 2 SETS, OR WORK ON ALTERNATE SIDES

Clean and press

This exercise is best done with either a body bar or a small weights bar (see page 14). You can also use your hand weights or simply do the exercise with no weights and still gain some benefits. The exercise works the muscles of the thighs – the quadriceps, hamstrings, and gluteus – along with muscles in the upper body – trapezes, deltoids, triceps, and latissimus dorsi.

1 Stand holding your bar – your grip should be just wider than your shoulders. If you are using hand weights (see page 14), hold them in line with your shoulders. Bend down to the floor, slightly sticking your buttocks out behind you and bending your knees as if you were picking something up off the floor. Look down to the floor as you do this to prevent any stress or tension in your neck and shoulder area.

2 Drive up out of this position standing tall with your chest lifted, allowing the bar or weights to rest just on your thighs with your elbows slightly bent.

3 Step back with the left foot into the lunge position; at the same time, bring the bar up to your shoulders. As you lift the bar up, keep your elbows tucked into your waist, and your hands in an over-grip position instead of an under-grip position.

4 Finally, follow through to extend the bar or weights to the ceiling as in the military press position (see page 57). Remember, when your arms are extended, your elbows should still be slightly bent. Repeat each step in reverse until you end up back down in the start position, squatting on the floor. Remember, as with the previous exercises, this should be one long, continuous move throughout each stage.

REPEAT 15 TIMES ON BOTH SIDES X 2 SETS, OR WORK ON ALTERNATE SIDES

Relaxation

These exercises have been designed to help you relax your body, either during or after your workout. The child's pose, for example, is a great exercise to add to your programme as a quick stretch and rest between sets, especially when you have been working the back or abdominals extensively, such as in the plank exercise (see page 77).

These exercises can either be done as a separate programme or to finish off your main programme. It is important to take time to relax and allow your body to realign back to its natural state to help prevent injury and soreness. Doing these gentle exercises will also help to give you a sense of wellbeing and calm after your workout.

Imagine driving a car along a road at 70 miles per hour, for weeks on end. What would happen if you never briefly stopped to check the oil and water, or to refuel? How long do you think your car would last

subject to this treatment? Now imagine your body is that car; exercise training and everyday living can have similar effects on your body, and like your car your body will work better and give a better quality performance if you allow time for cool-down and rest breaks.

These exercises have been taken from a yoga background, so while you practise the moves try to focus on quietening your body and mind. Draw all your senses inward, breathe slowly and regularly, and try to feel your muscles beginning to relax further with each breath.

The dead man's pose

This exercise is great for allowing your body to relax and rejuvenate totally. It may feel more comfortable to remove your shoes and socks first, but this is optional.

1 Lie on your back on your mat or a soft surface with your legs apart and feet rolling out to the sides. Place your arms just out to the sides. Have hands either palms up or down. Close your eyes and draw your attention inward so that you relax and become more attuned to your inner environment.

HOLD FOR 10 BREATHS – ALLOW YOUR FOCUS TO TRAVEL FROM YOUR FEET RIGHT UP TO THE CROWN OF YOUR HEAD

The child's pose

This exercise is great for relieving any stress in your upper and lower back. It may feel more comfortable to remove your shoes and socks first, but this is optional.

1 Sit on your mat on your heels with your knees together. Roll forward over your thighs, and rest your forehead to the floor, allowing your arms to spread out on the floor in front of you. Close your eyes and let go of any tension, especially in your back.

2 For a slight variation, take your arms around to your feet and place your hands palms up on your soles.

3 If you feel dizzy, light-headed, have high blood pressure, or if your buttocks stay high in the air and you feel like you are nose-diving, rest your forehead on a thick pad or stack your fists one on top of the other to rest your forehead on.

HOLD FOR 10 BREATHS, LONGER IF YOU WISH

The mountain pose

This exercise is best done at the end of your relaxation session. It is a wonderful one to centre and rebalance your body, as well as revitalizing it. Ideally perform it when you are barefoot, but this is optional.

1 Stand tall with your feet together. Squeeze your heels and thighs gently together so that you begin to feel the muscles in the thighs contract. Take your arms above your head, with your elbows slightly bent and your palms facing each other. Slide your shoulders back and down, drawing them away from your ears. Take a slow breath in, and at the same time, draw in your abdominal muscles slightly.

2 As you begin to breathe out, turn your hands around so that the backs are facing each other, and slowly begin to lower your arms to your side, drawing two large semi-circles either side of your body. Keep your thighs softly squeezing together and really try to reach away with your fingertips so that you feel your arms become very strong and the muscles working.

3 Finish with your hands by your side, softly pressing into your thighs. Stand tall with your chest lifted and your eyes looking slightly up, as if you are looking over the horizon. Breathe in and slowly reverse the move until your hands are back above your head in the prayer position.

REPEAT 5 TIMES – THIS IS A FLOWING, CONTINUOUS MOVE. ALLOW THE SPEED OF YOUR BREATH TO CONTROL THE SPEED OF THE MOVEMENT

Women's health

Women who exercise regularly are fitter and healthier than those who lead a more sedentary lifestyle – this has been proven in research by many health professionals.

This chapter looks at some common health issues that affect women throughout their lives. Pregnancy produces many different changes in a woman's body. By performing regular weight-training exercises, during and after pregnancy, you will reduce backache, tone your abdominals, ecourage good posture, and your pelvic floor will be strengthened, aiding the process of childbirth and postnatal recovery. You body will also remain fitter and healthier.

The pelvic floor

How to keep the pelvic floor strong is discussed because it is an important issue for all women, not just during pregnancy, but also in later life. The pelvic floor is a hammock of muscles that passes from the pubic bones in the front to the coccyx at the back. It fans out on either side to attach to the pelvic bones. The sling is divided into two halves to allow the urethra, vagina, and anus to pass through. The major support for the uterus and vagina come from the cardinal ligaments, uterosacral ligaments, and endopelvic fascia. Keeping the pelvic area strong also facilitates a speedier recovery after operations.

Training and the menopause

The menopause is a time when the female body goes through many changes which can prove debilitating and draining. Many women suffer with side effects of the menopause, such as hot flushes and night sweats. Once our ovaries start to produces less oestrogen, often beginning from the age of 45 onwards, the lining of the uterus eventually thickens and periods stop.

A small amount of oestrogen is still produced after the menopause by other glands and body fat. Women carrying slightly more body fat may have less symptoms; however, fitter women have also been shown to have fewer symptoms.

Doing regular weight-training exercises during this time can keep the body fitter, help reduce many of the unpleasant side effects caused by oestrogen loss, and increase bone mass, reducing the risk of the onset of osteoporosis.

Bowel control problems

The most common cause of bowel control problems is childbirth – as the baby passes through the vagina the muscles or the nerves near the rectum may be stretched or torn. Some women have short-term loss of bowel control right after childbirth. In other cases it may not show up until many years later. Also, as a person ages, the anal muscles may weaken. It can also be linked to the following problems: regular diarrhoea or constipation, certain medication, diabetes, multiple sclerosis or a stroke, inflammatory bowel disease, colitis or cancer of the rectum, and surgery or radiation therapy to the pelvic floor.

Irritable bowel syndrome (IBS) is a disorder of the intestines. No one knows exactly what causes IBS, but it often seems related to stress. Pelvic exercises are often used to help strengthen the muscles that surround the openings of the rectum, urethra, and vagina, and an increase in fitness levels has been shown to help improve symptoms of IBS.

Pregnancy and later life

Regularly exercising during pregnancy can have many benefits for both mother and new baby, and it can also keep you fit when you are older. But if you have not exercised before, check with your doctor before starting the weight-training programme (see pages 29–81).

During pregnancy a woman's body changes dramatically. By performing the exercises in the weight-training programme you can help your body to adapt and experience many of the following benefits:

- **Abdominal strength** – this is important to help support the weight of the growing uterus, act as a splinter to the spine, and help childbirth.
- **Stronger, toned abdominal muscles** – these are less likely to separate severely during pregnancy. If separation does occur, the muscles will realign more quickly in stronger abdominals.
- **Good posture and strong core strength** – this helps to control the amount of pelvic tilt, which naturally occurs as the baby grows.
- **Aids relaxation** – sleep is improved, but flagging energy levels are also increased.
- **Helps improve circulation to the mother and fetus** – this can also prevent varicose veins and leg cramps.
- **Reduces backache** – this common problem in pregnancy is improved by better posture and strengthening the abdominal muscles.
- **Faster postnatal recovery** – psychological wellbeing is increased. The feel-good factor is experienced from the release of endorphins, and self-image and confidence are improved.
- **Increases body awareness, particularly of the pelvic floor** – this enhances the mother-to-be's ability to relax this area and ease childbirth.
- **Increases venous return** – improved stamina helps different positions to be adopted for longer.

- **Aids joint stability** – this can help with carrying around increased weight during pregnancy.

Exercises to avoid

During pregnancy avoid the following exercises to prevent any problems. From 20 weeks onwards, don't lie on your back to exercise. This is because you may suffer with a condition called 'supine hypotensive syndrome'. This is where the weight of the uterus pressing on the great blood vessels (aorta and vena cava in the heart) may mean the baby does not receive enough oxygen, which could lead to complications.

From the second trimester, avoid any flexion moves such as sit-ups, crunches, or crunch twists as these may cause further separation of the linea alba.

Postnatal exercises

These can help realign the body to its former posture. However, no exercise should be started until at least six weeks after a normal birth or ten weeks after a Caesarean section. Below are some exercises to avoid:

- Flexion moves such as sit-ups, crunches, or crunch twists until at least 16 weeks after the birth. Then perform the diastasis test opposite before starting these exercises, because further separation of the linea alba may occur and stop the abdominals from realigning, leaving the spine at risk of injury.
- Do not over-strain or lift too much weight. Concentrate on your posture and retraining your body to return back to its pre-pregnancy state.

- Try not to do too much exercise if you are breastfeeding as it may make your milk dry up.
- During pregnancy your abdominal wall (rectus abdominus) will part to allow your baby to grow forward in your stomach. After the birth your abdominals should begin to realign. Before starting an exercise programme, check this has happened to see which exercises to avoid.

Testing for diastasis (separation of the abdominals)

Lie on your back, with your knees bent and your feet flat on the ground. Place two fingers below, at, or above your navel. Slowly lift your head off the floor – you should feel the two sides of your rectus abdominis close together between your fingers. If you can't, this generally means the gap is greater than two fingers and that diastasis is still present.

If it is still present, only do static contractions using the transversus muscle (see page 74), and pelvic floor exercises. Once the separation decreases to two fingers, begin to do low-level curl-ups (see basic crunch p.75). Wait until the recti sheaths have realigned and further strength has been regained before doing oblique exercises (see pages 78–81), as these may exacerbate the separation. When you start to do curl-ups, concentrate on not letting the tummy make a dome shape – this occurs in most postnatal women.

Pelvic floor and stress incontinence

Stress incontinence affects new mothers and elderly women, but also some keen exercisers. Perform regular pelvic floor exercises (see below) over several weeks. After childbirth you should notice a difference quickly.

Research shows that about a quarter of new mothers suffer from stress incontinence in the first three months after giving birth. For about 15 per cent this continues well into the first year.

Every time you jump, several kilos of abdominal organs go into the air with you. When you come back down, the weight of the organs and the pull of gravity put a strain on the tissues holding them in place, as well as the ligaments securing the bladder, bowel, and

womb. This affects the pelvic floor – the muscles that stretch from the pubic bone to the backbone. The pelvic floor has many functions. It:

- is an outlet for urination, defecation, and childbirth
- supports the contents of the pelvis and abdomen
- maintains continence of urine and faeces
- counteracts changes in abdominal pressure
- prevents prolapse

A strong pelvic floor can stop leakage from the bladder and bowel by the muscles staying slightly tense, unless you relax them by going to the toilet. If sudden pressure is put on the bladder by a cough, sneeze, or jump, the pelvic floor should react in time to prevent leakage. If it is weakened, the result is a spurt of urine.

Pelvic floor exercises

You can locate the pelvic muscle by pretending you want to stop passing urine.

Slowly pull up the pelvic muscles and hold for at least two seconds to start with, working up to 10 seconds. Repeat this movement up to 10 times. Next do some quick contractions of a second, repeating at least 10 times. Repeat both exercises at least once a day.

The menopause

After the menopause, the vaginal lining becomes thinner, dry, and less flexible. The drop in oestrogen also thins the lining of the urinary tract and weakens the tissues of the pelvic area, increasing the risk of stress incontinence. The most beneficial exercises at this time are ones that increase pelvic support, such as as abdominal movements (see pages 74–77).

As oestrogen levels decline, there is a higher risk of osteoporosis, which exercise can help. During exercise the ligaments stimulate the bones, increasing the production of osteoblasts (which build bone). Exercise strengthens the muscles that support the bones and joints, and reduces the risk of injury for women who are genetically more at risk of osteoporosis.

Oestrogen also protects women from heart attacks and strokes, so after the menopause the risk increases. But this can be reduced by exercising regularly, staying at your correct weight, and eating healthily.

Nutrition

Although exercise is a great way to burn fat and increase muscle tone and general all-round fitness, following a nutritious eating plan is also essential for maintaining your optimum weight and to stay healthy.

Healthy eating guideline

For optimum health *The Food Guide* suggests you eat foods from the five major food groups to get all of the nutrients you need.

The first group is **fats, oils, and sugar**. These are foods such as salad dressings and oils, cream, butter, margarine, sugars, soft drinks, candies, and sweet desserts. These foods provide calories and little else nutritionally, so only use them sparingly. Moderation is definitely the key with this group – the national recommendation for fat intake is 30 per cent of your total calorie intake.

The next two groups of foods are the **dairy and protein** groups such as milk, yoghurt and cheese, and meat, poultry, fish, dry beans, eggs, and nuts. These foods supply calcium, iron, and zinc, and you should aim to eat two to three portions from each group daily.

The next group is **vegetables and fruits**. Most people need to eat more of these foods for the vitamins, minerals, and fibre they contain. The aim is to eat between three and six pieces of fruit and vegetables a day – ideally five. Drinking a glass of fruit juice does count as one portion.

The biggest food group that provides us with most of our energy is **carbohydrates**. These are breads, cereals, rice, pasta, and all grains. You need between six and eleven portions of these a day. Wholemeal varieties contain more fibre.

The number of servings that are right for you depends on how many calories you need, which depends on your age, sex, size, and how active you are. Almost everyone should eat at least the lowest number of servings in the ranges.

Recommended daily calories

The suggestions for the amount of calories you need to eat daily are based on the recommendations of the National Academy of Sciences:

- 1,600 calories is about right for many sedentary women and some older women.
- 2,200 calories is about right for teenage girls and active women. Women who are pregnant or breastfeeding may need more.

Now, look at the table opposite. It tells you how many servings of the different foods you need to maintain your calorie level. For example, if you are an active woman who needs about 2,200 calories a day, nine servings of breads, cereals, rice, or pasta would be right for you, plus about 170g (6oz) of meat or other protein per day. Keep your total fat intake (fat in the foods you choose, as well as fat used in cooking or added at the table) to about 73g (2¼oz) per day.

If you are between calorie categories, estimate your servings. For example, some less active women may need only 2,000 calories to maintain a healthy weight. At that calorie level, eight servings from the grain group would be about right

What counts as one serving?

Carbohydrates – bread, cereal, rice, and pasta – 1 slice of bread, 28g (1oz) of ready-to-eat cereal, 1 cup of cooked rice or pasta

Vegetables – 1 cup of raw, leafy vegetables or other vegetables that are cooked or chopped, 1 cup of vegetable juice

The number of food servings needed for your calorie level

FOOD GROUP	1,600 CALORIES	2,200 CALORIES
Carbohydrates	6 portions	9 portions
Vegetables	3 portions	4 portions
Fruit	2 portions	3 portions
Dairy group	2–3 portions	2–3 portions
Protein (meat) group	141g (5oz)	170g (6oz)
Total fat	53g (2oz)	73g (2¼oz)
Total added sugar–	6 teaspoons	10 teaspoons

Fruit – 1 medium apple, banana, orange, 1 cup of chopped, cooked or canned fruit, 1 cup of fruit juice
Milk, yoghurt and cheese – 1 cup of milk or yoghurt, about 42g (1½oz) of natural cheese, 56g (2oz) of processed cheese
Protein – 56–85g (2–3oz) of cooked lean meat, poultry or fish, 1 cup of cooked dry beans, 2 eggs, or 1 cup of nuts

If you want to lose some weight, the simplest way to do this is to increase the amount of physical activity you do and reduce the fat and sugars in your diet. But eat at least the lowest number of servings from the five major food groups because you need them for the vitamins, minerals, carbohydrates, and protein they provide. Just try to pick the lowest fat choices from the food groups.

To gain weight, increase the amounts of food you eat from all of the food groups. If you have lost weight unexpectedly, see your doctor.

Good fat versus bad fat

Monounsaturated fats help to raise HDL ('good' cholesterol) levels and are found to be good for your heart. You can find such fats in olive oils, nuts, and avocados, for example.

Saturated fats, which contain LDL ('bad' cholesterol), should be limited. These are not healthy fats for your heart. You will find these fats in food such as red meats, cheeses, and lard.

What about cholesterol?

Cholesterol and fat are not the same thing. Cholesterol is a fat-like substance present in meat, poultry, fish, milk and dairy products, and egg yolks. Both the lean and fat of meat and the meat and skin of poultry contain cholesterol. In dairy products, cholesterol is mostly in the fat, so lower-fat products, such as skimmed milk, contain less cholesterol. Egg yolks and organ meats, such as liver, are high in cholesterol. Plant foods do not contain cholesterol.

Dietary cholesterol, as well as saturated fat, raises blood cholesterol levels in many people, increasing their risk of heart disease. Health authorities recommend that dietary cholesterol be limited to an average of 300mg or less per day. To keep cholesterol at this level, follow the above guidelines, keeping your total fat intake to the amount that's right for you.

It is not necessary to eliminate all foods that are high in cholesterol. You can have three to four egg yolks a week, including those used as ingredients in custards and baked products. Use lower-fat dairy products often, and occasionally include dry beans and peas in place of meat.

Fluids

It is recommended to drink about 2 litres (3½pt) of water a day (or one glass an hour) to flush out waste and toxins. Aim to keep your alcohol intake down to the suggested 14 units (one unit is equivalent to a small glass of wine or half a pint of beer) a week for women.

Index

Names of individual movements are indicated by **bold** type